Voi

A Sacred Anthology for Today

Voice of Many Waters

A Sacred Anthology for Today

Compiled and edited by

Kay Snodgrass

Geneva Press

Louisville, Kentucky

Scripture quotations, unless otherwise indicated, are from the New Revised Standard Version of the Bible, copyright © 1989 by the Division of Christian Education of the National Council of the Churches of Christ in the U.S.A., and are used by permission. Quotations marked (KJV) are from the King James Version.

Acknowledgments will be found on page xvii.

Book design by Running Feet Books
Cover design by Pamela Poll Graphic Design

First edition
Published by Geneva Press
Louisville, Kentucky

This book is printed on acid-free paper that meets the American National Standards Institute Z39.48 standard.☉

PRINTED IN THE UNITED STATES OF AMERICA

00 01 02 03 04 05 06 07 08 09 — 10 9 8 7 6 5 4 3 2 1

Library of Congress Cataloging-in-Publication Data

A catalog record for this book is available from the Library of Congress.
ISBN 0-664-50111-7

Dedication

This book is dedicated to the glory of God and in appreciation to the contributors represented in this anthology, who create from a love of God and others, and a dedication to art. Special thanks go to Mary Duckert, John Purdy, and Marci Whitney-Schenck (publisher and editor of *Christianity and the Arts*), mentors who helped me get in touch with a number of writers and who have given much helpful advice and encouragement from the beginning of this project in 1997. My grateful thanks go to Thomas Long, director of Geneva Press and my gracious "boss" at *These Days* devotional magazine, for his early and continued encouragement and guidance. Finally, my heartfelt gratitude goes to my family, especially my husband, Jerry, without whose patience, support, and "patronage" this book would never have been compiled or published. My children Elissa and Grant are the poems I cherish most of all. I thank them for the gift of themselves.

Contents

II. Waters of Growth and Community

III. Waters of Pain and Death

IV. Waters of Restoration

Tributaries

Foreword

$\mathcal{E}$ rnest Hemingway said that a novel should be like the tip of an iceberg, persuading readers that the author knows vastly more about the characters and setting than appears on the printed surface. Surely you are at least vaguely aware of the vast labors concealed beneath the surface of any printed work—in addition to the writing itself, including compiling, design, editing, proofreading, typesetting, and publishing. For *Voice of Many Waters*, this labor (in the initial version) was undertaken by one person!

Definitely, Kay Snodgrass did not shoulder those labors for financial reward. I know, I know, writers admonish one another with Samuel Johnson's adage, "Only a blockhead writes except for money." And Jesus himself said that "the laborer deserves his wages." But I think Kay did it all for love—love of the printed word, love of the Word made flesh.

Hemingway was right. Samuel Johnson was half right. And who would dispute Jesus? But certainly William Shakespeare was wrong to write of "Love's Labor Lost." What is done for love will profit many.

John C. Purdy

Preface

The heavens are telling the glory of God;
and the firmament proclaims his handiwork.
Day to day pours forth speech
and night to night declares knowledge.
—PSALM 19:1–2

And I heard a voice from heaven, like the voice of
many waters, and like the voice of great thunder; and
I heard the voice of harpers harping their harps. And
they sang, as it were, a new song before the throne . . . .
—REVELATION 14:2–3, KJV, ALT.

Early in human history, our "primitive" fathers and and mothers—whose lives were so short and full of toil—created images, stories, songs, dances, and poems that expressed their world of spirit and flesh. They understood art to be much more than mere trinkets added as decoration to their lives and faith after all other needs were satisfied. They knew intuitively that people and communities need art.

Sister Wendy Beckett, contemplative nun and arguably the world's most popular museum docent, says, "Art is about being human." Art and a perception of the spiritual perhaps truly define humankind and set us apart as creatures made in the image of, and for the glory of God. Sacred art results from the creator in us communing with the Creator of us. And it is made, possibly even mandated, to be shared. This anthology reflects the belief that, of all ways of knowing, art may be freest to explore and express the Spirit that lies at the heart and soul of our being.

When one early Christian named John — imprisoned on the barren island of Patmos — beheld his vision of God and of heaven, he expressed it through symbols, drama, and the cadences of poetry. This art was then rendered into English exquisitely by the translators of the King James Version (KJV) of the Bible. Though modern scholarship makes newer translations more accurate, none surpass that version in the artful use of language. Doubtless the artistry of the KJV helps account for its viability even after nearly four hundred years of its use. And who can say what part that artistry played in spreading its message? For John, the language of art provided the only means vivid and insightful enough to make sense of and convey the revelation that grew out of his suffering and worship as he was caught up "in the Spirit on the Lord's day" (REVELATION 1:10).

Artists of faith, like John, can stand even in the heart of darkness and see beyond the horror, into the Light. Creating and participating in art are essential ways of discovering and conveying truths by merging the senses with the imagination. Like lightning bolts across a dark sky, poetry, paintings, parables, and all of the arts can reveal whole new vistas. Like dreams, they can bring forth symbols and stories from the recesses of our psyches. Raising fundamental questions, art takes us deeper into an understanding of ourselves and others. And, just as important, art imprints truths upon our hearts forever through sensual joy.

Some indicators point to an increasing awareness in our culture of the value and necessity of religion and art. Public television has aired programs such as Bill Moyers's series on Genesis and Sister Wendy Beckett's overview of art, which have attracted wide audiences. Moreover, excellent magazines such as *Christianity and the Arts** often feature spiritual, artistic endeavors that point to a renaissance of art in the religious community.

When you read the biographies of the contributors in the last section ("Tributaries") of this book, you will see that the artists represented here come from varied backgrounds and beliefs. In addition to a dedicated pursuit of writing and other arts, most of the contributors pursue other careers and activities, often of service to others within a religious context. It is likely they would all feel kinship with the first poem in this anthology, "The Salt and the Light," by Linda Malnack, in which she pens these words: "I write the way I love: writing, loving, it is all the same. . . ."

The works in this volume have been grouped somewhat arbitrarily by the themes of (i) creation, (ii) growth and community, (iii) pain and death, and (iv) restoration, rather than by artist or genre. Many of the works could have gone into several categories; others stubbornly defied exact categorization. The wide array of works present a mixture of styles, viewpoints, and even accessibility—some being so complex as to possibly perplex the reader who is not willing to take the time to dig deeper or to accept that not every word can be "explained," others so simple that the reader may be tempted to skim and miss the depth found in their humble simplicity. Yet I believe exploring these basic themes through the varied eyes of poets, painters, musicians, storytellers, essayists, humorists, and even clowns enriches our lives. My prayer is that by looking through their artful and spiritual eyes, you will gather new insight and will experience afresh the living presence of God's glorious, creative Spirit in your own life.

Kay Snodgrass

*For information about this magazine, write to *Christianity and the Arts*, P.O. Box 118088, Chicago, IL 60611; call toll free 1-877-245-1993; or e-mail chrnarts@aol.com. Web site: www.christianarts.net.

Acknowledgments

Grateful acknowledgment is made to the following for permission to quote from copyrighted material.

HarperCollins Publishers for excerpts from *The Longing for Home*, copyright © 1996 by Frederick Buechner.

Kairos for "Overflow" and "October," copyright © 1996 by Jean Janzen. From vol. 1, issue 2 (fall-winter 1996–97).

Deanotations for "Untitled Offerings on Poetry," "Noticing Water," "Water from Stone," "Small Blessings," "Untitled: I have gotten better," "Untitled: The Romans invented telephone poles," "Tricks or Treats," and "Untitled: I will climb the highest mountain," by Dean Blehert, publisher of *Deanotations*, a magazine of poetry by Dean Blehert.

Inklings, for "Falling into Sky" (1977) and "a daughter's terrain," by Gretchen Sousa (1996). Used by permission of Brad Hicks, publisher.

Monday Morning, for "One to One," by LauraGrace Eisenhower, from vol. 52, no. 13 (August 1987), copyright 1987 by Presbyterian Church (U.S.A.), a Corporation. Also for "Next of Kin for Three Persons," by Shirley Klotz Bickel, from vol. 63, no. 6 (March 23, 1998), copyright 1998 by Presbyterian Church (U.S.A.), a Corporation.

Faith at Work, for "The Cardiac Ward: A Place for Clowns?" by Bud Frimoth, from the winter 1996 issue.

The Christian Century Foundation, *The Christian Century*, for "At Work on the Sabbath," by Kate Benedict, in the March 6, 1991, issue. Copyright 1991 Christian Century Foundation. Also for "A Singing," by Ivy Dempsey, in the June 19–26, 1996, issue. Copyright 1996 Christian Century Foundation. Reprinted by permission.

The Presbyterian Layman, periodical of the Presbyterian Lay Committee, for "Savor," by Bard Young.

Eight Studies for Senior Highs, for "Sonnet I" and "Still Light," copyright © 1997 by Lois Kilgore. Originally published by the National Teacher Education Project, 1977.

The National Library of Poetry, for "The Lost Word," copyright © 1995 by LauraGrace Eisenhower, from *East of the Sunrise*, edited by Cynthia Stevens (Owings Mills, Md.: National Library of Poetry, 1995).

Voice of Many Waters

A Sacred Anthology for Today

I. Waters of Creation

In the beginning God created the heaven and the earth. And the earth was without form, and void; and darkness was upon the face of the deep. And the Spirit of God moved upon the face of the waters.
—GENESIS 1:1–2, KJV

Then at the beginning, there was no nonbeing; neither was there being. There was neither the earth, nor the sky, nor anything beyond. . . . There was no difference between night and day. There breathed the One, breathless. . . . All this was unknowable, covered by water, the empty, and the One.
—Paraphrased from various translations of "Nasadiya" (Hymn to Creation), Hindu hymn in the Vedas

Linda Malnack

The Salt and the Light

I let lift
and fall my water-colored pen
dipped
in thought, trickling little letters
of light
before light lifts on the edge
of my day.
I write gleaming jots and tittles
not so holy,
I know, as those writ in the Holy
Writ, but I
write the way I love: writing,
loving, it is all
the same, ripples and froth across
a white page
sprung from the still-water slough
of life's gathered
force. I will the words to puddle
or sing
or swing their green way like rapids
down a river
to the sea that I may see at last
or at last
be joined with all the rollick
of the multitude
and mix my chemistry with the salt
and the light

of the ocean's most plausible applause
clapping
against the fine white shoreline
of heaven.

Frederick Buechner

A Secret in the Dark

Scripture: LUKE 24:13–32

*I*n Florida, in the winter, there is a walk that I take early in the morning before breakfast most days. It doesn't go to Emmaus exactly, unless maybe that's exactly where it does go, but in the literal sense it takes me some three miles or so along a completely uninhabited stretch of the inland waterway that separates the barrier island where we live from the mainland. I do not know any place lovelier on the face of this planet, especially at that early hour when there is nobody else much around and everything is so fresh and still. The waterway drifts by like a broad river. The ponds reflect the sky. There are wonderful birds—the snow-white egrets and ibis, the boat-tail grackles black as soot—and long, unbroken vistas of green grass and trees. It is a sight worth traveling a thousand miles to see, and yet there is no telling how hard I have to struggle, right there in the midst of it, actually to see it.

What I do instead is think about things I have been doing and things I have to do. I think about people I love and people I do not know how to love. I think about letters to write and things around the house to get fixed, and old grievances and longings and regrets. I worry and dream about the future. That is to say, I get so lost in my own thoughts—and *lost* is just the word for it, as lost as you can get in a strange town where you don't know the way—that I have to struggle to see where I am, almost to *be* where I am. Much of the time I might as well be walking in the dark or sitting at home with my eyes closed, those eyes that keep me from recognizing what is happening around me.

But then every once in a while, by grace, I recognize at least some part of it. Every once in a while I recognize that I am walking in green pastures that call out to me to lie down in them, and beside still waters where my feet lead me. Sometimes in the way the breeze stirs the palms or the way a bird circles over my head, I recognize that even in the valley of the shadow of my own tangled thoughts, there is something holy and unutterable seeking to restore my soul. I see a young man in a checkered shirt riding a power mower, and when I wave my hand at him, he waves his hand at me, and I am hallowed by his greeting. I see a flock of white birds rising, and my heart rises with them.

And then there is one particular tree, a tree that I always see because it is the northernmost one I come to and marks the spot where I turn around and start for home. The label on it says that it is a Cuban laurel, but its true and secret name has nothing to do with labels. It has multiple trunks all braided and buttressed and roots that snake out over the ground as widely as its branches snake out into the air. Here and there, it has sent a slender air root, which in time turns into another trunk that supports its weight like a sinewy old arm. There are one or two places where the leaves have gone brown and brittle, but the tree holds them high into the sky as proudly and gallantly as it holds the green ones.

At the risk of being spotted as a hopeless eccentric, I always stop for a moment and touch the coarse-grained, gray bark of it with my hand, or sometimes with my cheek, which I suppose is a way of blessing it for being so strong and so beautiful. Who knows how many years it has been standing there in fair weather and foul, sending down all those extra trunks to keep itself from breaking apart, and wearing its foliage like a royal crown even though part of it is dying? And I think it is because of that quality of sheer endurance that on one particular morning I found myself touching it not to bless it for once, but to ask its blessing, so that I myself might move toward old age and death with something like its stunning grace and courage.

"When I was hungry, you gave me food, when I was naked, you clothed me," Jesus said. "When I was a stranger, you welcomed me."

And "When I was a tree," he might have said, "you blessed me and asked my blessing."

Kathleen Long Bostrom

Canticle to Creation

"Let's see, now where do I
   begin?"
Swirling, shapeless,
   empty, faceless
   darkness everywhere.
"Light! That's good!
   I'll call it Day
     and separate it from the Night.
   Enough for now."
The First Day ends
As perfectly as God intends.

The Second Day dawns through the deep:
   Flowing, gushing,
     flooding, rushing
   water everywhere.
"A hollow dome
   will now divide
     the waters up from those below.
   Now sky is born."
So ends Day Two.
The earth is bathed in shades of blue.

Day Three begins, all wet and clean:
   Cloudy, foggy,
     misty, soggy
   dampness everywhere.
"Land shall appear
   from mountains tall
     to deserts, beaches spread with sand.
   But that's not all.

This day's not o'er:
I've set the stage for something more."

"Upon the land let green things grow":
  Seeding, sprouting,
    budding, flowering
    lushness everywhere.
"Ripe fruits hang thick
  from every branch
    and vegetables of varied type.
  How good this is!
My spoken Word
Has now completed this, the Third."

Day Four unfolds so soft and still:
  Glimmer, gleaming,
    shimmer, beaming
  brightness everywhere.
"Signs to mark
  the passing time,
the sun, the moon, and stars all shine
  and take their turn."
Day Four is done.
And closes with a setting sun.

"Fish and birds I now call forth":
  Swimming, diving,
soaring, flying
  movement everywhere.
Fly high above,
swim deep below,
then fill the earth and multiply
  and spread the word:
"The earth's alive!"
And so concludes a full Day Five.

"Wake up! Arise! Day Six is here":
  Running, leaping,
    crawling, creeping
  creatures everywhere.
"Beasts of every
  kind spring forth
    from grandest to the very least,
  both wild and tame.
Now all's in place:
It's time to form the human race."

"I've saved the best part for the last":
  Living, breathing,
    thinking, dreaming
  people everywhere.
"My image shall
  reflect in you,
    for through your life I sanctify
  all that I've made.
I've done this much
Because you are my crowning touch."

"One favor I shall ask of you:
  Guard, protect,
    adore, respect,
  and keep my world in peace.
Care for this earth,
  watch over life,
    make sure that all are treated fair."
Day Six is through
And makes God smile;
"I think I'll rest a little while."

The Seventh Day completes the week:
  Rest, refresh,
    spirit and flesh,

for God has blessed this day.
"These words of mine
have made a world:
    with all I see, I am well-pleased.
      Now time begins,
But I'm not done:
My work on earth has just begun."

Jean Janzen
Overflow

Today the young swallows
are practicing their flights,
streaking in and out

in frantic patterns
from their mud nests under
the bridge. Their cries echo

over the high water of the creek,
an urgent calling from their silken
bodies, like an overflow.

Once we saw a tourist's version
of *Swan Lake* danced on a stage
so small, the principals repeated

their patterns in tight circles.
And at the end, the need and joy
collapsed for lack of space.

Our stories are too big
for our bodies. Our first heartbeat
is spillover, and we are born

in a rush of water and cries.
With our whole body we lift
our first vowels to the air—

a stream, pressing
from a place we do not know.

Dean Blehert

Untitled Offerings on Poetry

There IS a place for poetry: After the Hunger Artist
starves to death, there is a brief delay while his
body and filthy straw are replaced by fresh straw and
a snarling tiger. Meanwhile, to avoid dead time,
a poet is invited to read.

———

It is easy for me to get confused with the poet
who wrote me: We both speak the same words. But I, the
poem, have a much clearer understanding
of what I'm saying.

———

Poetry is communication devoutly to bewitched.

———

Judith Deem Dupree
High Desert Sunrise

The morning is a womb,
a shaped silence,
like the way He places things
invisible around us.
Not a muffling. No, the air
is free of cloy and ripe
with the rhythm of sage come into bloom.

God has stirred the bush ahead;
it burns with early light.
And lo, His fingerprint is pressed
against the nubby oak;
a squirrel deciphers it too quickly
for my dull eye.

The grasses unbend, drink up
their meager draught,
plumping their veins against the sun—
knowing every shadow of its fierce ascent,
the lap of its hot tongue.

But for now the sky is cool
to a solemn sweetness, and unfolds
like a great wing spreading,
like the infinite shape of the soul
in its final rising.

Kathleen Long Bostrom
Summer Snow

*T*he community where I live is built around a lake. The houses, once consisting solely of summertime homes, have gradually expanded and filled the winding streets. Grand new homes take their place alongside dwellings that were born as humble cabins. The acres surrounding this community are rapidly becoming overrun with new housing developments that stretch in every direction.

One thing in particular sets my community apart from all those fancy complexes: the trees. In all the new communities, there are few if any trees. The ones that have been planted are small and frail. But in Wildwood, trees abound. Majestic oaks and maples shelter homes and yards, providing welcome shade in the summer and piles of flame-colored leaves in the fall, much to the delight of children and the chagrin of those who rake. Graceful evergreens provide splashes of color in the bleakness of winter, and when the snow first falls, the green needles are iced with white frosting that turns the entire neighborhood into a fairyland. Springtime brings new life as buds and leaves unfurl and blossom and fill the world with hope.

Each morning as I walk, I drink in the trees. I marvel at their thick, rough trunks and powerful roots breaking through the earth. Branches are as diverse as hands, some slender and smooth, others crooked and gnarled. They lift my eyes up off the ground and direct my attention to a broader empire. We are friends, the trees and I.

One early morning I walked my usual path, around the lake and down a quiet street. As I turned the bend, something in the air caught my eye. A snowflake, then another, then dozens more, floating silently on a gentle breeze. Soon the air filled with delicate white puffs. Stunned, I reached out and caught one in my hand. My surprise came not from the snow, for I have seen this beauty before. But this was a Saturday morning in June, and the air far too warm for winter folly.

The snow as it turned out, was not made of icy crystals, but cottonwood seeds. A tree somewhere, or perhaps two or three, had given birth to thousands of offspring, tiny seeds, carried by tufts of cotton parachutes to varied destinations. One lawn, blanketed in white, appeared to be the maternity ward of the cottonwoods. I stopped walking and stood in the midst of this summer snowfall, enveloped in nature's gift, seeds of new life, new beginnings.

As I went my way, I pondered what had at first appeared to be a miracle, but had turned out to be only a common act of nature. Then I stopped, and glancing back across my shoulder at the air still freckled with white, I wondered: Are fragile tufted cottonwood seeds rising and falling on the breath of the morning any less a miracle of God than snowflakes in June?

The earth brought forth vegetation: plants yielding seed of every kind, and trees of every kind bearing fruit with the seed in it. And God saw that it was good. (GENESIS 1:12)

Bard Young

Epiphany

"What is poetry that does not save nations and people?"
—*Czeslaw Milosz*

"Però salta la penna e non lo scrivo." *
—*Dante*, Paradiso, *xxiv, 25*

With studied application,
the sort required of scholars and mechanics,
of farmers late in season, fearing winter,
of priests perfecting oblation,
with such intensity of commitment
a poet writes his continuing will and testament.

History, once thought dead, sadly moves—
while steeped in cause the poet shoves
beyond his mind all thoughts of lily fields,
the work of worms in soil on steamy nights,
the dark accretions in the rings of trees,
the songs of doves.

Morality, the ethics of the thing,
concern for justice, issues touching mercy,
matters all intrinsic to the soul
matters rolling, rolling in the mind of God—
the poet visions these and thinks aloud,
"Poetry should weld us, make us whole."

Meanwhile, dawn lifts, burning.
Motes invisible by night now fire
the air, and droplets perfectly create the world
inverting and suspending all his rage.
The poet's pen leaps up.
He cannot force its point to touch the page.

Therefore the pen leaps up and I cannot write of it.

Edward Wier
An Atheist on the Beach

They say it all just happened with a bang,
Then time and chance took over after that.
From nothingness it all just somehow sprang,
Coincidentally, with a habitat,
From single cells, then on to three and four,
We struggled up the ladder sans a guide,
Relentless in our effort to be more,
With natural selection at our side.
What odds we must have beat to find our fate!
And then achieve the wonders we have wrought.
What windfall brought us to our present state,
Of self-aware imaginative thought?
While much obliged, his grateful mind went blank,
As he walked on with nobody to thank.

Dean Blehert

Noticing Water

Just over this grassy slope appears
different stuff, called *water* or a *lake*—
of no or any colors; keeps moving toward us but
    gets
no closer; seems all one thing, one huge rippled
    whole,
no matter how many pieces of it are removed;
    gives
way to a finger's softest touch, but smashes flat
tons of a crashing airplane; has a surface that
    repairs
penetration instantly—Oh, it's different stuff,
this stuff of which dirt, grass, and people
largely consist. How did it get away from us,
    becoming
so thoroughly itself?

Meat is mostly water. Blood is mostly water.
Green vegetables are mostly water.
Even a few of our rivers are still
mostly water.

If bodies are 92% water, this lake could be
    converted
to 92% of an army. Someone should tell
the Pentagon.

Though my body is 92% water and 98% liquid,
I am careful to dry it after a shower,
and I always wear dry clothing.
Perhaps we developed such habits
so that we can more easily detect leaks.

Time for tea.
I am already 92% water,
98% liquid. The rest
is delicate china.
I float in my body, flavoring it,
the tea bag.

After shampoo,
a Chinese dragon of suds
coils on the water.

Exxon casts oil upon the water, ancient
compressed ferns, dinosaurs stretch out
upon the ocean, taking over again.

I am as unknown as water,
rejecting all light or passing it through
almost untouched, just slightly bent.
In me you see a distortion of yourself
or you do not see me at all.

I'm here to see the ocean—ran
all the way! Have I missed anything?

Water poured into a leaky bucket,
loss is the life we continue to give
what is no longer able to receive it.

The bumper sticker says:
"Water—Our Most Precious Resource.
    Conserve It."
No—next to each other, what we must not waste
is words. Even now it is harder for me to tell you
you are precious.

Whoops—poured lukewarm water
on my tea bag and wasted its savor—
like sex without cherishing.

The beach sifts through my sealed fingers,
once rock and shiny shell,
now—after how many millennia
mulled in the mill of wind and water?—
a powder too fine to hold,
time showing off.

"Stop!" cried puddle to sun—
"You're dazzling me! I can't
stand it any more!"—and
ran away into the sky
to hide in a cloud.
Boy so intent on pissing—
tries to cover the water with bubbles.

I do grow wise with age:
Now I always check for
unrinsed soapy armpits
before I leave the shower.

Nose running, eyes tearing for days
on end. Only 98% liquid? It's a lie!
soon, like the Wicked Witch of
the West, there'll be nothing left of me
(sniff! sniffle!) but a pile of
pajamas and a sopping wet hanky.

My love, we are 98% liquid,
this sleek, solid flesh an illusion—
but good to the last drop!

Dean Blehert
Untitled

The ocean keeps
thrashing up waves
to become mountains, falls flat,
tries again, undaunted. Nearby,
the mountains, having made it,
are bored stiff

Edward Wier

Playing with Words

He lifts her sloping body to his chest,
With silver threads well taut and tuned to play.
They soon will quiver as she wakes from rest,
To speak soft sounds no words will ever say.
His fluid fingers find their measured mark,
And feel for missing music waiting there.
She breathes with glowing colors in the dark,
Ascending and descending through the air.
Around her neck, the strings of pearly notes,
Now sail beneath his tame and trembling face.
They disappear like seaborne drifting boats,
While others billow out to take their place.
   I taste the fading foam that can't be caught.
   And turn the ebb back into waves of thought.

Bard Young
The Three Philosophers

"The world is round, or so it seems,"
said the true empiricist.

"It's round by God's almighty means,"
proclaimed the Catholic lyricist.

And then the man of reason spoke —
how steady-voiced, how level-eyed.

About him flowed his lengthy cloak
as to the crux his mind applied:

"The world is round, I think; therefore
I am convinced I must be right.
Believing less by knowing more
I quite transcend all mortal light."

With lyrical empiricism
both opposed their friend, of course:

"We think, sir, and we wish no schism,
you've put Descartes before the horse."

Neil Ellis Orts
Summer Pondering

Samuel lay on his back in the grass, the full length of his ten-year-old frame stretched out. Above him were brilliantly pink crepe myrtle branches, the blooms brought alive by a buzzing swarm of golden honey bees.

"Whatcha doin'?" asked Samantha, his little sister. He hadn't noticed her until she plopped down beside him.

"Watching bees," he said.

Samantha scooted on her back so her head was next to Samuel's. "Aincha scared of em?" she whispered.

"No, Doofus," he said. "They're more interested in the flowers. If we don't bother them, they won't bother us."

"Oh." The two lay quietly for a few minutes, lost in the bees' steady hum. "What are you thinking about?" Samantha asked. She knew Samuel never stayed quiet this long unless something was on his mind.

"Stuff," he said.

"What sort of stuff?"

"Important stuff," he said, trying to sound much more than two years older than his sister. "You wouldn't understand."

"I would so," she answered. "Tell me."

Samuel, not in the mood for arguing, started thinking out loud. "Well, okay. There's all this stuff that's out there that can hurt us, and there's all this stuff that guards us."

"Like what?"

"All kinds of stuff. Like, our skin is like a wall between our guts and germs in the air. And the air, it protects us from stuff in space. Stuff falls into the atmosphere, and it burns up before it hits us."

"Yeah?"

"Yeah. And last night, on the news, you know in that Science Minute thing they do, well, they said that maybe earth has life because of where it's at in the solar system. All the planets outside the earth's orbit protect us from big stuff in space. You know, like that comet that hit Jupiter a while back."

"Oh, yeah," Samantha said, as if she were following Samuel's train of thought.

"Kind of makes you wonder," Samuel said as he scratched his leg. (The grass was making him itch.) "How much stuff is out there guarding us? And if all this stuff is out there guarding us, why do we still get hurt sometimes?"

Samantha decided not to ask any more questions that day.

Edward Wier

Reasons to Live Below

I want to glide my hand across
The horse's velvet coat.
And feel the sheets of muscle
Beneath the tightened hide.

I want to taste the swirling waves
Of salt-spray in the sun.
And breathe the spell of surging seas
Underneath the azure sky.

I want to hear the haunting hiss,
As rain rips through the leaves.
And watch the mist of damp night creep
Below the marbled clouds.

I want to wrap myself around
The scent of fresh-cut grass,
While falling into fragrances,
Under cool and shifting shadows.

I want to see the color shoot,
Out from the clouds and gems,
Never returning to the source,
Or arriving at the goal.

Shirley Klotz Bickel

Memories of Eden

Luscious hips undulate
the beat of incessant rap
boy-man and newly bestowed woman
taste the forbidden

is it quenchless lust
or fresh-picked love that
electrifies their senses
throbs juicy lips
tangles bodies
intoxicates reason
grinds restraint to the ground

the freshest fruit
is quickly snatched
slightly tasted
then flung aside
as spotlights ignite the
darkness
quick as a snake strikes
they grab their clothes
to hide their nakedness

days have slithered
into months
he's been lured to other faces
new fruits to pluck
barely sample then discard
as he crawls in the grass

far away in a smelly clinic
her dignity shaved
exposed to whoever enters
her lips twist and quiver
to garden memories
agony accelerates
no one dabs her sweat or blood
once succulent lips beg for
ice
under the lights' intensity
she cries
"Help me, Somebody, help me,"

"I must be dying,"
she writhes

at last, with a gushing sound
a new blossom opens.

LauraGrace Eisenhower

Sonnet to Dawn

Blue-black horizon hills outline the view,
Silhouette against the eastern mauve of sky;
The promise growing lighter, brighter, new;
The rapture of the dawn's exploding cry
Of ecstasy, of joy, crimson now and gold;
We're given a moment's glimpse of heaven's bliss;
To south and north soft cumulus clouds unfold,
Now blushing pink at their Creator's kiss.
Mourning doves and meadowlarks awake
And chant melodious odes to greet the day;
Earth yearns and turns, anxious now to shake
All shadows of the brooding night away.
Why should I ever sleep and miss the sight,
God's saying once again, "Let there be light!"

Shirley Klotz Bickel

New Axis for Time

Dragging with unborn child
panting with each ascent
stripped of friends and family
turned away by those suspecting the worst
steadied by a man who finds it hard
to see where all this is leading.

No clean place to lie in
Bethlehem's town of strangers.
Resting goats inertly chew their cud.
Bleating mother nurses her lamb.
No midwife to keep watch,
only vision of holy imperative.
Such loneliness mingles with
nearness of God.
No angels make it easy.

Groans and screams, then startled
cries announce a new life.
Unruly joyous tears bathe
the baby's face.
Jesus child inhales relief
in mother's swaying arms,
hushed by father's astonished gaze.
Flies torment the resting donkeys
who never bother to rise or kneel.
Such a Holy advent in
a lowly place births
hope for every trusting race.

Trina Zelle
Untitled

A perfect circle
of embrace
mother and child
in a new moon curve of heart
against the clear
blue sky
Come and drink
calls the moon
to her starry children
above the bare
thorn trees
O milky face, O star eyes
echoes Mary
Come and drink

Gretchen Sousa
Falling into Sky

It was dusk,
the light fading fast.
I was drawn to the ocean
by a sunset already in afterglow.
At the edge of the cliff
I nearly fell into sky—beauty-struck.

> The evening star, bright gem,
> pinned heaven's plunging depths
> to a point of light.
> One sweeping cloud,
> like a desperate angel in flight,
> raced after the sun. A half moon
> already announced the coming of the night.

I stood there
lost in deep familiarity,
a nostalgia
more resonant than I have ever known—
the recognition of an ancient home
beyond eternity, a threshold I knew
from some dim memory . . .

> A tern flew across the horizon
> high above the water,
> the attenuated light of the moon
> glittering on its white wings.

Bard Young
Peggy's Ars Poetica

Her eyes cross slightly beneath half-open lids,
that sleepy, self-effacing look Down's children have.
Her gaze is always just beyond
the edge of common ground—
as when some shore bird's errant navigation
yields horizons of open solitude
unbroken by a purple point of land.

She walks across a field not wondering
from where or how the snow came in the night,
sees the feathered tips of broom sedge
deeply rooted in soft white earth
as nothing like the dormant grasses
brownly nesting there a day ago.

Just how she knows the brooded world—
hatching out of nothingness
her palpable and friendly universe—
seems less like reasoned human plan
than dancing sparks beneath God's beating wings.

She runs in awkward inefficient gait—
pigeon-toed, flailing elbows
pitching her unbuttoned coat
from side to side across her back—
runs the orchard slope to witness
scarlet apples leap from snow-ridged limbs
and wing downwind to gleam on distant trees.

THE STORY BEHIND "PEGGY'S ARS POETICA":

Peggy O. Peek (July 20, 1929–February 11, 1996) was my wife's maternal aunt, the baby sister who was born with Down's syndrome. When Peggy was born, the doctor informed Peggy's parents that the child would not live a year if removed from a special-care institution. In those days, children with Down's seldom lived long. Her parents' response was, "Oh, yeah? Watch this." They took her home and made her the center of the family's life (among five other brothers and sisters). Peggy never acquired speech, could not sing, could not dress herself, but she radiated affection; she was a magnet for every grandchild and great-grandchild of the family. When Peggy's parents died, two of her sisters assumed care of her. One of the sisters is my wife's mother. Peggy would spend a month or so with one of the sisters, then go to the next sister's home for awhile. My wife and I visited her often; she taught us how "simple is beautiful."

LauraGrace Eisenhower

One to One

I wonder if ever among the One in Three
One asked another One, "How does it feel
To walk with time and flesh our little earth;
How does it feel, my Son?
        And could he tell
The barefoot feel of grass fresh wet with dew;
The splashing of the sea upon the sand;
Sudden breeze with honeysuckle laden;
To human ears the meadowlark's entreaty;
To human eyes the daisy-covered hill;
To climb with young-limbed strength the hoary oak;
Or stretch oneself to rest in its cool shade;
To watch as poets watch a thousand skies,
And never ever see them twice the same;
To know the earthly rapture of the dawn,
Earth's turning, yearning, reaching out for light;
And then when day is done, to know as well
The softness and the blessedness of night;
To remember the tenderness of mother's touch;
To walk as boy with other boys, as man
With other men and women; know devotion
As earthly love, prerequisite to heaven?

And would He say with thankfulness, that this,
To have known both earth and heaven, and to be
Both God and man, is His eternal bliss?

Dean Blehert
Water from Stone

Language, in dead mouths,
turns to stone. This explains
why poets hack and hammer words
into unfamiliar forms: to
surprise language into hectic life:

If you strike the rock, you get water,
but you never get to enter
the promised land. We are commanded
to speak to the rock simply.
It is alive and will respond.

II. Waters of Growth and Community

For I will pour water on the thirsty land,
   and streams on the dry ground;
I will pour my spirit upon your descendants,
   and my blessing on your offspring.
They shall spring up like a green tamarisk,
   like willows by flowing streams.
— ISAIAH 44:3–4, NSRV

"If we have not learned to serve humankind, how can we
serve spiritual beings?"
   —Confucius (551–479 B.C.)

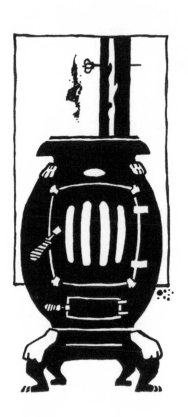

Jean Janzen
Kindling

First sounds are first light,
translation for the shifting face,
the wall from which he drinks.
Pitches and sibilants become names,
unlocking doors. And when
the father murmurs, "my child,"
rubbing the boy's scalp until
it sparks, he hands him
match and kindling. Amazing
that we hold such fire,
that we are trusted with it.

And that child rouses
in the pre-dawn dark, even
as his father sleeps, descends
the stairs and reaches into
the cold, black mouth of the stove.
He blows his name over the first,
small flames, not only for his own
deep shivering, but for others when they rise.

Trina Zelle

Church Women United

I remember the backs of their heads,
white waves disciplined tight
under fine hair nets,
sitting on hard pews
in an airless church
on July days as hot and still
as the nineteenth-century heaven
reproduced on their handheld
funeral parlor fans,
swung with the precision
of a slow metronome.
On their backswing
I would catch a glimpse
of golden light filtering
onto the backs of cows
standing knee deep in green rivers,
surrounded by lush primeval trees.
As I waited for release
in the damp stillness of silent prayer
there was nothing in the world
but those fans and the wisp of cool air
that would find me
if I sat just right.

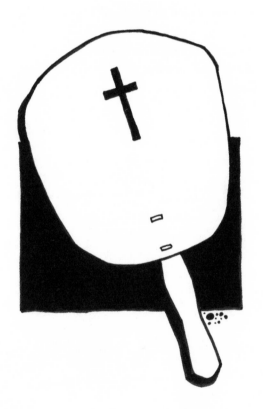

Trina Zelle

John the Baptist

This strange child
of their old age
didn't laugh much.
Small hands dry
as the sandy soil
in which he played
with single-minded urgency,
he would hug his old
mother and stare down
the shimmering road
over her shoulder.

Bard Young

The Jars

He moves in backward glide against the wall—
a little peace, some anonymity
amid the throng of thirsty wedding guests.
And then, before his mother says a word,
his eyes fall on the jars. They, too, stand in
the shadows of the wall—empty, open,
waiting to be filled. His fingers touch
the rim of one, feel the curve of clay,
its smooth and useful strength, like bone.

Before he's asked he sees the jars accept
the water poured and poured, the jars all filled,
a flood beyond all need, beyond abundance.
He grips a jar's smooth rim and hears the rush
of tributaries coursing to the rivers,
feels the churn of tides beneath the moon,
sees in the jar's dark reflecting pool
the history of the world. "Is this enough?"
And then his mother: "Son, they have no wine."

Frederick Buechner
Silence

When I was teaching at Lawrenceville, I had the feeling that my life was disordered, directionless, and somehow shabby, and a friend of mine told me about an Episcopal monastery on the banks of the Hudson River, where there was a monk who he thought might be a good person for me to go see because he was a wise and good man. So, off I went in my car to that monastery, full of questions—there's a kind of wonderful divine comedy about all of this—and when I got there, I found this particular monk, whom I'd been sent to see, had taken a vow of silence, and wasn't seeing anybody. I've felt since, that the great value of those three days, in that monastery, was the silence. If I'd found the monk and asked my questions, he would have answered the questions, and that wouldn't have solved anything. I've often thought if God had said to Job, "All right, I'll tell you why these terrible things happened. Here it is . . ." and had given him six typewritten pages, it wouldn't have solved Job's problem either, because like me, he wasn't after answers. He was after something else, and what the silence said to me was, "Be still, and know that I am God. . . ."

Trina Zelle
Called

Fifteen, and your
worn-down boot heels
scuff tattoos of longing
on the dance hall floor
Eyes shift restless
lighting on everything
but what you really want

Already a priest,
your hands pass
through the darkness
reach elbow deep
into that hunger
lift out
its ragged heart
still beating

You drink,
and God's dark
wine staggers you
down your years
while the faces
of your children,
lovers, distant
landscapes slip by
while your aching flesh tracks
its heart's longing
to a high
and empty place

Mary Duckert
What Is Life For?

*T*he memorial service was a time to remember. It didn't make my skin crawl or my teeth itch. We gathered at the Town Hall, and because the sun was out, we went to the Firemen's Park and assembled on the baseball diamond, looking up to the highest point in the village. We sang and prayed and praised God for what we know of life. The pastor, a scant thirty, asked us to go home and talk over the question: What is life for? He read from Deuteronomy and Luke to give us a clue or two. He shook hands with me and clasped my shoulder afterward and said, "Thank God you have your writing."

So now I'm home with no one to talk over the question he posed. But the fellow is right about one thing: Thank God I have my writing. There were times these last few months and weeks, particularly, as I witnessed joy and hope supplanted by boredom and hanging on that I was grateful beyond words that I was born to write. Not writing in this journal in reaction to the state of affairs or state of my mind, but writing for other people.

I remember one day when I was eight years old standing alone on top of the hill we stood below today. I could see ten miles in every direction. If I'm going to write stories for people, I'm going to have to see more than this, I told myself. I told my parents, too, and it became part of family lore. The day they showed me Lake Michigan for the first time I asked, "Is it just like where we're standing, on the other side?"

"You have to imagine that," my father said. "You're the writer in this family. You can do that."

"I can make something up, sure," I persisted, "but I can't see that other side. It has to be there. This is a lake not an ocean."

"The last time I was on an ocean," my father began correcting me, "I was very sick. I would have been even sicker if I had thought it was so big it didn't have another shore. Just because you can't see land doesn't mean it isn't here."

My mother said to us, "You know what I think is over there? A girl your age asking a mother and father our age, 'What's it like on the other side?'"

I couldn't get much writing accomplished today between telephone calls and drop-in visitors. Dorothy Lund's advice on my life as she sees it tells me more about her than she knows: "Don't try to make something up to sell right now. You'll have to call on your faith at a time like this. Writing in your spare time is OK after you heal."

My faith and my art coexist. Neither is in a closet. Everything I write is autobiographical. Even writing a recipe or directions from the airport reveal something of who I am. My faith is not unconsciously autobiographical. It is yoked to purpose, and for me that is God's purpose for all of us on earth or anywhere else in creation we may turn up. I never ask: What is life for? The life I live is a constant answer. What I do is in the interests of others. Nobody writes, paints, sews, saws, chisels, or takes photographs twenty-four hours a day. But in all we do, we reflect our purpose—our faith, our reason for being.

There was an obituary in the paper of a photographer for the old *Life* magazine. The writer described the man as a self-acknowledged loner. He had looked through the man's photographs and found anguish, terror, and self-satisfaction but no interaction. I wonder what that artist would have said his life was for. We are all created for purpose. When one of us dies, the community meets to give thanks for that life, to comfort those who will miss the person most—and most of all—to go on to face the water without seeing the other shore.

Sara Covin Juengst

Memories

Swinging the shine of my Mary Janes,
I sat in the family pew trying hard not to squirm:
    twisting my smooth-brushed hair,
      tracing with my gaze the carvings on the high-backed
        chairs
      (elaborate curls like garish eyes,
      crosses, trefoils, lovely geometrics).
I liked the quiet wood,
    the polished organ pipes,
    the radiance smiling through colored glass.
I leaned my head on Mother's shoulder
    and let the alliterative points of the pallid sermon
    drift through my mind.
My father cleared his throat and leaned forward
    to pray in earnest solemnity.
Bored, yet awed,
    wanting to be somewhere else,
I was somehow glad
    to be in the assuring presence
    of family,
    friends,
    and, mysteriously,
      God.

Neil Ellis Orts
Candor

The pastor arranged the pens on his desk while he waited for her to speak.

"I'm sorry, Pastor," she said after a silence. "I thought it would be good to share this. It may be. But I can't."

"Sure you can. This is a safe place."

"To an extent." She relaxed into the chair a little, but her fingers still clung to the armrests. "But some secrets might best remain unspoken. Maybe some secrets aren't meant to be shared. Even with your pastor."

"Believe me. I am neither shocked nor repulsed by anything humanity does. I've seen too much, done too much to sit in judgment. But confession is good for the soul. Don't carry the burden."

She sunk lower in the chair, her chin digging into her collar bone. "If it were just me—but if I told you everything that's bothering me—it involves other people. People I love. People who I don't want you to think less of. The secrets aren't all mine to tell."

"But the truth will set you free."

She looked up at her pastor. "Jesus said, 'I am the way, the truth, and the life.' I don't doubt that. Knowing Jesus, assures me that this moment doesn't bind me. I have hope of moving beyond this moment." She swallowed. "I know something about being free in Christ."

"What, then?"

"It's the facts that bind me. The facts have consequences. To know the truth behind a situation is freeing, but the facts can imprison. I don't want to imprison anyone else by spouting facts in the name of truth."

The pastor looked out his office window and silently studied the cardinal at the bird feeder there. Finally, he said, "I have written many sermons that I will never preach. They revealed too many facts about me. About my parents. About my friends. I couldn't—not even in proclamation of the gospel. Not even in the name of truth."

Her eyes widened. "Then you understand?"

He looked down at his hands and picked at a hangnail. "Yes." His clichés and quick answers fluttered happily away with the red bird.

She took a deep breath and stood. "Thank you, Pastor." She went to the door. "I'll see you Sunday." Then she flew away also.

Left alone, he smiled. "The awful humanity of it all," he muttered. He, too, felt lighter.

Dean Blehert

Other Silences, Other Voices

Walking through the park,
I pass with embarrassment
a ragged man who talks loudly
to no one I can see.
Is that the way I sound
to passing angels
who can hear my thoughts?
And in what stillness dwells
the being who can hear
the incoherent babbling
of angels?

Angels

Angel—from a Greek word
meaning *Messenger*. We each
came here with a message
for all the others,
could not speak each other's languages
(each had his own),
garbled each other's messages
in desperate attempts to translate,
to understand . . .
gave up, forgot.

Hence this hell
full of fallen angels.

When any man rediscovers
what he has to say,
he can no longer remain
merely human.

The remembering alone
makes an angel, the saying
a poet.

Bud Frimoth

The Cardiac Ward: A Place for Clowns?

*I*s the cardiac ward a place for clowns? An obvious answer to the question would be, "No. The people are too sick and shouldn't be bothered." But since I've spent a week there on two occasions, I thought it might be just the place to go as a clown.

The idea for this scenario took place in September 1995, after my second trip by expensive taxi (ambulance) to the hospital. My cardiologist said this time open heart surgery was the best option.

As I was recovering from that surgery with all of the dopey sensations and wondering about life and living, I felt a very strong urge to come back when I was well enough.

Now another part of the scenario: Both my wife, Lenore, and I have been doing nonverbal clowning since 1978. We've done services of worship, clowning in schools and nursing homes and parades and have even clowned for the birthday of a young Saudi Arabian child in the royal family.

Teaching "Clown Funshops" has been one way we've helped birth new clowns. You can never have enough clowns! But our way is not the noisy, outrageous, stunt kind of circus clowning. God loves them, too, because they work hard at their trade. What we teach is "relational," nonverbal clowning. With this type, the clown seeks to bring out the "little child" in the other person without the distraction of words—a "child" that may be hurting deeply inside.

The clown also attempts to be vulnerable to an "audience" of one person or a hundred while being open for acceptance or rejection. As a clown, one is obvious in crazy grease-painted face and outrageous outfit. The audience may be in a church pew, a care center, or along a parade route and loves the personal attention the clown gives to each. The clown simply relates by tickling a smile out of people, by stooping to polish their shoes with a toothbrush, or carefully scrutinizing the little pinkie of their left hand. In this way the clown shows

a deep awareness of them as real persons to whom the clown can give one-on-one attention.

Knowing this background, you may begin to see why I wanted to return to my cardiac ward. There nurses, doctors, aides, and room attendants treated me tenderly as they helped restore health. I just *had* to return to show my thanks for their efforts as well as bring a bit of joy to patients.

Every other week, Lenore and I visit most of the rooms on the cardiac ward as "Wrinkles" and "Zyppurr." I chose the clown name Zyppurr because many open heart patients refer to their 10- to 12-inch scar down the center of their chests as a zipper. Just what do we do? First, we clear the visit with the nursing staff, who guide us to the patients needing our attention. Then we simply knock at the patient's door. When welcomed in, we share a little skit using some paraphernalia which I had been given when I was recovering. The main gadget is one used for expanding the chest, —a breathing device that is a must after chest surgery. I suck in my breath, using this device, and then blow it out on a pinwheel attached to the gadget.

Next Lenore gives the patient a simple pinwheel she has made. Almost immediately the patient tries to blow, an often difficult experience. But when it is accomplished, big smiles cross the patient's face and those of family members in the room. We gently applaud their effort.

A small, triple-folded tray sign is also given the patient with these words written in bold calligraphy:

Welcome to the OOHH's
The Order of Healing Hearts
Zyppurr the Clown,
A Graduate of the Cardiac Ward
Wrinkles the Clown,
A Cancer Survivor

"You've been through this?" they ask. I nod. "Then there's hope for me." The patient has caught the message without a word from either Wrinkles or Zyppurr. Just as we leave the room, I show them a sign on the basket that holds my gear: "Laughter—God's gift of healing to humanity." You can find that gift in some of the most unusual places, including rooms on 2G, the cardiac ward of Providence Hospital in Portland, Oregon.

Bud Frimoth

Looking for Turkeys

It was a simple call on my answering machine:
>"There are 14 wild turkeys coming up the hill towards
>   my house;
>if you're around, c'mon over and enjoy their beauty."

The wonder of creation's presence
>When you take the time to look;
Her intuition had Joan turn from her reading and look out
    her window,
>and there she made the wonder-filled discovery,
>but she didn't keep it to herself;
>>a phone call was made
>>an invitation given . . .
>>>to share in the grace of the moment.

Another conversation
>that same day:
>>"I was in the city the other day and saw two robberies
>>   in broad daylight
>>in two different places,
>>>and in each incident
>>two older couples were involved.
They had carefully guarded their walking,
>staying close to each other
>with the woman's handbag on the inside between them;
Yet five young men surrounded them,
>two from the back and two in front,
>one simply pulling the man backwards
>>while the other grabbed the purse
>then all of them running off . . . not too swiftly . . .
>>gloating in another show of their manhood."

Janet just had to share that observation
    about the wonder of shadows as they affect our lives
    and make us overly cautious . . . only to lose even then.

I ask you Lord—
    "Which of these is the way, the truth, and the life?
    Why do you seem so absent in our days and nights—
    Where are the people who are trying to turn this
        around—
        is it only the devil who revels in delight
        at the darkness—even in broad day light?"
Jesus—
    You loved the outcast;
    you sheltered and encouraged those
    whose lives were most devastated by darkness;
Why not now?
    Are we the only ones you trust to do your job?
    If so, then we've certainly messed up a lot these days.

————

Help me to look for turkeys—
    and then share the wonder—
        I might even discover You are there!

WHAT IF...   EVANGELISM

"Look at this. We raise beans and carrots.
 They raise goats and sheep. Why don't
 we widen our membership circle?"

"Good idea. It'll be better for
 Family Night Dinners. But,
 what'll we call it?"

"How about... Evangelism?"

Dean Blehert
Small Blessings

Blessed are the bees, who swaddle their babes in wax and cram them with sweetness.

Blessed are the ants, who, in their orderly swarms, ease themselves over and under each other without malice, each willing to be a way for others.

Blessed is the spider, who, flightless, yet unwieldy on land, weaves an element of its own, nor earth nor air, where it, alone, can dance.

Blessed is the caterpillar, who endures for months a slow, blind, many-footed trek from leaf to leaf all day to nourish a few brief days of glorious-eyed flight.

Blessed are the flowers, whose beauty serves no purpose of their own, for bees are colorblind.

Blessed is the wasp, who lets me capture him in a cup and help him outside, then zips away with renewed energy and does not sting me.

Blessed is the worm, who mates with another worm even though he/she is sufficient unto him/herself.

Blessed is my old dog who, unable to stand, yet licks my face, even though I, who know everything, refuse to tell him why this is happening to him.

Blessed is the cat, who forgives me when I toss her soft unmoving gifts into the woods.

Blessed is the rabbit, so still on the path ahead to
    remind me that I am dangerous.

Blessed are the starlings, who fill up the trees just when they begin to have vacancies.

Blessed is the cardinal who tears open the dullest day by
    tugging on a bright red thread.
Blessed are the stones I tread, for they hold the universe
together with their faith in gravity, while I indulge in
levity.

Bard Young
The Visitor

The way I knew to use the hall,
her room was on the right, down near the end,
lights always on, door open wide—
always straight and neat, precise and shining,
like her.

"Come in, come in, young man. I'm always glad
for company, though I don't have much time."

Her usual comment was no long-term look
toward death—but just the short-term truth.

"I have so much to do. I never seem
to finish what I plan.
Last week I had six letters I was sure
I'd finish 'fore the week was out.
Didn't.
That added one to this week's list.
Guess I could have put it off,
But that old soul sure needs to hear from me
just now. Her marriage is a constant grief
and she stays worried for her only grandchild."

So she'd talk to me in great detail
trying hard to fill me in
on all the heartaches she could surely mend
if God would only spare her, spare her time.

She spoke as if I knew or ought to know
those folks; I felt it,
felt that somehow I should know.
And when I left, I always hoped

she'd find the time to write to all
the poor souls on her list, hoped that God
would grant more hours in the day, the week,
so this small ancient woman, straight and neat,
precise and shining, could mend and mend
and let me feel once more, when I would say
good-bye, that she had mended me,
That she had been the visitor, not I.

LauraGrace Eisenhower

The Word

—MATTHEW 25:29

once to my searching soul there came
   a word
      and a word
      and a word
the first word said come
   see starlit dew
      and glint of sun
         on feathered wing
and sign of petal opening
   and rapture of the dawn
hear melody of muted string
   and sing

     the second word said
       but no
       sit here in the gutter
         and in the dung
spread it over yourself
   and revel in it
      and spoon-feed it to your young
for this is what the world is
   avarice
     greed
       lust
         war
hate life
   and tear the fetus from the womb

the third word said
   to the first word, come
      receive
         and be blest
for to him that hath shall be given

and to the second
   the third word said
      hush, hush you and die
for from him that hath not
      shall be taken

Kate Benedict
At Work on the Sabbath

At work on the Sabbath, shunning church to kneel
instead on these cold tiles, scrubbing
scummy tub and rusty faucet, rubbing
beads of sweat from neck and brow, I feel
a reverence still. To clean what has become tainted!
Surely it's a kind of consecration,
this dipping and lifting, this squeaky ululation
of suds through mop and sponge. Soon each painted,
each porcelain surface will be lit up, born anew.
Ammonia vapor circles me like incense,
a sacramental of this busy rite: It's penance,
adulation, absolution at once! One true
Lord, today I spurn your house solely
to restore my own. But it's your day. I keep it holy.

Linda Malnack

Going Home

For Tim

Some days I see Tasmania in your eyes,
the Leven River churning into Bass
Strait past Picnic Point and Turners
Beach. I see your sworn determination
to return—someday—to the stillness
of stones, that shore where your father
and the brothers from Gospel Hall waded
into waves fully clothed, and you watched
them press against the current deeper
and deeper—chest-high, chin-high—net
strung like hope between them, pulling.
You want to return as they returned, net full
of flounder, mullet, to fill wheelbarrows
as they did, showing off their bright silver
currency to wives and children. But you
have no fortune, only the fact of your survival
and Jesus, and the father who still fishes
for you, throwing prayer over the wide
expanse of water. Your mother, even, casts
lures of letters, parcels filled with violet
crumble, newspaper clippings. That's when
Tasmania is greenest in your eyes, those hills,
the gorse- and wattle-lined tracks. Soon,
your dad will snag us all—you, me, the tiny
daughter we have spawned—and reel us in.
He'll get that smile, the widest he allows
himself, and mumble, "Good on ya, son,
good ta have ya back." He'll load us in his
heshin bag and take us home for tea.

Jeanne D. Wandersleben

Gift to Japan

A *True Account*

*T*he year is 1931. America is in the grip of the Great Depression. Herbert Hoover is president of the United States. American isolationism is a popular stance. Interest in foreign affairs is directed mainly toward Europe.

On the other side of the globe, Japan penetrates ever more deeply into China. This news draws a routine ho-hum from most Americans, who basically distrust and dislike all Orientals—Japanese, Chinese, Koreans. They consider Japan a "funny little country" where people bow to one another, eat strange food, live in paper houses. Japan is viewed as a string of blobs and dots on the map "somewhere out there" in the Pacific. Americans have little chance to know personally any Japanese, who, with other Orientals, have been barred from entrance into the United States since the American Immigration Act of 1924.

In August of 1931, a ship sails from the west coast of America bound for Kobe, Japan. Aboard are Americans with various interests in the Orient. Among them is a missionary, returning to Japan for her third term as a teacher in a small denominational school. Her name is Edith Husted.

The journey takes nineteen days. Edith looks forward to returning to the school where she has been a teacher of music. The school is a small one dedicated to training young Japanese women in ways of doing Christian social work in Japan. As part of their training, they must learn music—how to play and sing and lead music from the Congregational hymnal, at least. How better to spread Christian belief and practice?

Back home, Edith's nine-year-old niece, Jeanne, is fascinated with her "Japanese aunt" and looks forward to the weekly letters that her aunt will write to her family. It is her grandmother who will read these letters aloud, and will say each time: "These letters are so interesting; they ought to become a book."

From Kobe, at Thanksgiving time 1931, Edith writes:

I suppose it's useless to comment on the Manchurian tangle at this long distance. Of course you who know something of Japan besides what the military clique are putting over on us, know that "we Japanese" do not want war, and that Christians all over this land are tremendously stirred to prayer over the situation. There never was a time (was there?) when there was so much deep sentiment for peace in the midst of an atmosphere of war. . . .

In 1932 Franklin Roosevelt is elected President of the United States. The country is divided over involvement in Europe. In many ways it is an idealistic age. Airplanes are becoming, not only interesting toys, but a likely means of international transportation. "Lucky Lindy" has become a hero in Japan as well as in other nations of the world since his famous solo flight across the Atlantic. Top world news commentators express outrage over the kidnapping and murder of Charles and Anne Lindbergh's baby boy.

Of secondary news value to the west is Japan's seizure of Manchuria, renamed Manchukuo, and ruled by a Chinese puppet emperor under control of Japan's military party. In Japan the Emperor Hirohito presents his new-year poem to the nation. It reads:

In prayer pleading
To the god of heaven and earth
     For a world without a wave,
     Calm as the sea at dawn.

Educated in the west, Hirohito is himself a peace-loving man with no personal desire to be a monarch. If he had his way, he would pursue the career of a marine biologist. He and his cabinet embrace "liberal" trends that, mainly in urban areas, represent a "new Japan," eager to take her place in world affairs. However, he and his cabinet

Edith Evelyn Husted
1892–1988
Courtesy of the Author

fail to exhibit strength against the escalating power of the military, who surely and steadily are taking over the government.

The military "clique" play on the disenchantment of a reactionary generation, suspicious of liberal, mainly Western, trends that seem to threaten traditional family and social values. In the minds of many people, Japan is still a sacred land watched over by lesser gods, and her people semidivine. Are they not ruled by a god—their divine emperor, the direct descendant of the Sun Goddess? They owe a debt to their mythical homeland, and thus they see death in the service of their emperor as a glorious atonement for their obligation. A still more glorious atonement would be the domination by Japan of all of eastern Asia. And eventually, of the whole world?

Countering these trends are Japanese Christians, among them Toyohiko Kagawa, whose approach is twofold: remedy economic conditions in Japan through cooperation; promote nonviolent beliefs and practice in international relationships. In a letter, Edith quotes a lesser known Japanese—a pastor who says in a lecture she attends:

> "Many Japanese say, 'For me to live is my country, or my Emperor,' but we must have a higher allegiance."

She comments, "It means something to say that out here, believe you me!"

In July 1937 Edith plans to visit her relatives, missionaries in China. Just before she leaves Japan, she writes:

> The newspaper extras yesterday report a scrap in Peiping that gave us all a turn, and I wondered whether I should buy my ticket. But today reports all things arranged peaceably. . . . I didn't buy a round trip ticket, because I thought I could tell better when I got there which way it would be best to come home. . . .

Back in Japan, propaganda proclaims the beginning of "A New Order in Asia." Patriotic fervor flourishes. Old legends of military might are invoked. The "Kimigayo," an ancient court song, is revived as Japan's national anthem. The Rising Sun, Japan's national emblem, flies over all, reminder of Japan's "unique place in the sun." All this is done in the name of a god, the Emperor, for his glory, and for the sake of "inferior Chinese," whose country they brutally overrun and pillage in order to create eventual peace. It is their "war to end wars."

Edith can hardly restrain herself from speaking against the blind patriotism stirring in her adopted country. Her pacifist viewpoints permeate her life, her teaching, her letters. As a pacifist she believes that in the midst of war, the Christian's task is to combat war hysteria, to resist the spread of totalitarian psychology, and to oppose legislation that promotes increase of armaments or the curtailing of civil liberties. "It is a terrible thing to be a consistent Christian in these times," Edith admits.

She writes guardedly, numbering her letters to her family, so they will know if they receive them all. Occasionally she sends a letter by someone traveling to America. Throughout her letters she insists: "The worst thing about war is not that the aggressor might triumph, but the hatred and suspicion that war engenders."

Speaking out becomes ever more dangerous as the military party takes over the minds of people. To demonstrate her beliefs, Edith takes up residence in the dormitory with the girls she teaches. One of them was to say of her later: "She was special. She not only taught us. She lived with us. She learned to think as we thought. But she brought us so much more. She showed us how to live as Christians in a nation where most people are not."

My grandmother kept most of Edith's letters, and so it was I who inherited them. Some sixty years later, I took up the task of re-examining the weekly communications that had so intrigued our family. In her letters of the 1930s, Edith's message of Christian pacifism is clear. Beyond that, Edith Husted emerges as a delightful person, viewing herself with humor, in spite of all that is occurring. Truly she was a gift to Japan.

The book of her letters, *Gift to Japan*, was published in 1996, thanks to a grant from International Communications Foundation in Japan, who saw in the book's contents a message of understanding between Japan and America. The book is now a gift back to Japan, a view of history that many Japanese have almost forgotten. It is also a gift to American readers who know little of the Japanese people previous to the war years.

Edith's words about war are true. Much of the hatred and suspicion engendered by World War II persists still, prejudices born of reluctance to see that each of us is the product of our own unique backgrounds with their myths about how it was and how it ought to be.

My grandmother's words about the value of Edith's letters were also true. They have finally become the book that she thought would be important.* I think she would be pleased. I think Edith would be pleased too.

* *For ordering information about* Gift to Japan, *write to Pacem Press,* 2345 *Eastern Ave., Alliance,OH* 44601.

Kay Snodgrass

The Cost of Fundamental Litigation

Come to terms quickly with your accuser
while you are on the way to court . . .
—MATTHEW 5:25

If I sue you because I'm *certain* of a thing you reject,
And you counter-sue because you're *certain* of its
    contradiction,
Is Truth served?
If I produce 100 witnesses, and so do you,
To echo our warring certainties,
Will Its case grow stronger?

What if I call up a star witness named Martin Luther,
And you respond with another named Anne Frank,
Each to swear on our own Holy Writ to certain certainties
    that cannot coexist,
What court can contain two witnesses so grand,
And who could be their judge?

But while we're supposing,
Let us imagine that right next door, another plaintiff
    stands,
Presenting yet another case of certainty,
A Texan who named himself David,
A certain man who worshiped himself to death in a garrison,
Should you and I postpone our own litigation to watch his?
(To be blunt, could we stop trying to push each other out
    of Heaven long enough to heed a case from Hell?)

Oh, maybe for a moment we might stop,
Distracted by an aging Lucy Sky-Diamond who sits cross-
    legged in the hall,

"All of you are right," she coos
(breathe in, breathe out)
"Everything is Good," she chants
(breathe in, breathe out).

But then, you point back to that Waco David
as your eyes meet mine.
"God, help us," you whisper.
"Amen," I add.
Our words rise and hang in silence
like incense, as we stand side by side.

Could moments like that *between you and me —*
Could something that simple really be
Insight enough,
All the certainty we need
To agree with each other while we're on the way?

Lois Kilgore

Sentences

Her sentence finished, she cleared her throat
And said,
"I've been sharing this with a few people lately."
I waited. The phone line crackled.
"I'm coming out to you because I know you'll accept me.
I'm a Lesbian."

I looked out the windows at the mountains and wanted to
cry.
So many mountains.
"I've already accepted you," I said, unable to think of
anything else to say.
We went on to speak of other things.

Later, heart lagging, but trying to deal with labels,
Wondering why she had told me,
Half wishing she hadn't
Because now I had to think of her as Lesbian
Before Friend.
Then I wondered if she thought of me as Heterosexual
Before Friend.
I certainly never told her that.
I didn't have to.

Then I began to understand.
It wasn't about me, or even labels.
It was her need to say, her need to be.
She accepted me.

Edward Wier

The Secret Scent

Soft skin soothes my frequent fears
While waves of words lap 'round my ears
Reaching past the hard-packed shore
Bidding me to love, adore

I find your face the fairest frame
Along the garland of your name
We are one, each other's plan,
Touch becomes God's very hand

Your love comes as a secret scent
The sparkle of an ornament
A fervent fragrance never fading
An atmosphere, always persuading

We plunge into the sweet, dark night
I close my eyes as we take flight
and know that nothing can defeat us
As the wild winds dance between us

I wrap myself around your waist
Then follow you from toe to face
Watching as you sweetly sleep

Edward Wier

Cosmic Irony

Bought a book called *Disappointment with God*,
Which was suggested to me by a friend.
I thought the bold title seemed a bit odd,
But I was too far from faith to pretend.
I thought that I perhaps could find some clue,
To the mystery which had restrained me,
Get back on the track and again pursue,
The path of hope which once entertained me.
I started to read in search of the cure,
Or some comfort at least for this lost sheep,
But found my ambition was premature,
When, after three chapters, I fell asleep.
   I dreamt I saw God revising his plan,
     Reading a book: *Disappointment with Man*.

Bard Young

The Smallest Things

At first they offer uninsistent questions
like, how many make up this visible segment?
By drawing nearer, how many can I see?
With better light, might I tease out more?

The hairs that coat the undersides of certain
leaves, the tiny barbs of flies' legs,
the rising bits in smoke, or Pinatubo
falling, piling on my sill as soot.

More and more they urge closer viewing.
To concentrate my vision and concern
requires rigor, a spiny mental state
that keeps at bay the howling macro world.

Not air, but microns, floating dust. Not water,
but light-absorbing particles. Not food,
but membranes, sinews, seeds. Not desert famine,
but grains of quartz, salt crystals left from tears.

Bard Young
The Oldest Things

The size of cosmic things determines age.
Fleeing galaxies spray from hot centers—
by miles in millions, by light years, parsecs—
sleeplessly expanding, away, always,
creating only distances between
corpuscles burning in a spacious body
of failing gravity, exploding in silence.

Not like an old rabbi
whose shrinking bones suck wrinkles in his skin
like troughs pulled in against gravity,
his brown gabardines wrinkled down
retreating legs, hiding collapsing socks.

Some oldest things are cosmic troughs,
the smallest, youngest ones they say
155 million parsecs long
and getting longer while we sleep.

He slowly walks with measured step,
each the interruption of a fall,
likes to sit facing the bright window.
Beneath the thin blanket,
his fingers interlace. He often sleeps—
head drooping, almost vanishing.

The window darkens. Galaxies appear,
exploding and exploding, old as God.

Gretchen Sousa
Morning Light

. . . the arrow endures the string,
to become, in the gathering out-leap,
something more than itself.
—RILKE

The screeches, alarms, sirens
and other raucous voices of the night
subside as morning light
creeps into my fractured sleep,
flickers across the room
in kaleidoscope patterns, dims
when low clouds win back their domain.

Call me, call me
into that still space
where the ennui of waking diminishes
and I arise
holding my life in my hands—
this luxurious hour
to read, to write, to pray,
to see the shimmering river of life
flowing by.

To stay in this place is everywhere:
cocoon, vista, womb, throne.
Then, quivering, I am ready
to be an arrow placed against the string,
and trusting, to be sent,
my oldest sufferings leaping out
to bear fruit, to become something more—
love, finding its mark.

Shirley Klotz Bickel
Longings for the Messiah

Scrapbook of days, new page —
soundless darkness, six A.M.,
and virgin air lure me to linger,
but I scan the headlines
and tiptoe indoors disturbed by the news.
Setting coffee mug aside,
I shuttle my diplomacy,
untangle children from
dreams of sleeping-in and canceled school.
Our dancing moonbeam only grumbles
through cereal nibbles.
Brothers chew on football scores
and injuries, usurp each other's
shirts — surprise, surprise.
Daddy's tea is swallowed with lumps
of news — Congress Probes Disputed Vote Fraud.
Record Set for Murders.

As I hurry past the torn chair
defaced by deceased cat, I wish
there were no ugliness or pain.
I long to touch the Holy, but see
no burning bush. Did Mary and Joseph
wonder why the same responsibilities
year after year? Did herdsmen
yearn for something beyond the rocky
pasture — some verdant meaning besides
being a sentry
for sheep?
By eight, all showers have ceased.

Everyone has found clean underwear and socks.
The last one has softly slipped into
the new day.

I turn on the CD and hum the refrain.
Such a mystery it is that Christ
was born to common folk.
In the laundry room I drop into a basket
clothes to hang despite the frosty air.
Why put on boots, wade through mud,
chill my fingers to hang up the wash?

An upside-down squirrel nibbles
from the bird feeder.
There are no angel visitants, no glorias,
but God is nearly touchable,
like the pine tree guarding
our house. How is it that God
discerns just when I need a fresh
infusion of his presence?
There's no stable nor burning bush
but somehow God's mercy speaks
through good-bye hugs,
trespassing squirrel,
and sheets flapping in the wind like wings.
In the mire of mundane duties
God reminds me to take off my boots
for "this is a holy place."

LauraGrace Eisenhower

Thoughts on Plowing
—*LUKE* 9:62

"No man who puts his hand to the plow and then
looks back is fit for the kingdom."

But find me another field, Lord . . .

Perhaps this field will never be green,
And this is a rusty plow;

That field over yonder more promising,
And some other time than now.

Then I remember, the Kingdom waits,
And no looking back will allow.

Lord, walk beside me, help me keep
My hand upon this plow.

III. Waters of Pain and Death

Save me, O God; for the waters are come into my soul. I sink in deep mire, where there is no standing; I am come into deep waters, where the floods overflow me. I am weary of my crying. My throat is dried; mine eyes fail while I wait for my God.

—PSALM 69:1–3, KJV

Birth, old age, disease, and death cause us pain. Grief, lament, dejection, and despair cause pain. Disappointment in not getting what we want causes pain. Briefly put, the five classes of grasping through our senses are full of pain.

—The Buddha, *Samyutta-nikaya* 5:420 (paraphrased from translations)

Judith Deem Dupree
The Wide Sea Eats

The wide sea eats voraciously;
it swallows up the sky
and gnaws upon implacable boulders,
spitting them out as sand.
The sea dribbles spume down its gritty chin;
from such froth we are born.

We are the blood, the cells, the great wash
of the sea,
and it is the spill, the amnion
from which we rise, salted with Hope,
shrugging off our scales
and gargling air,
thrusting forth our tongues and fragile fingers.

All life
belongs to the sea—
to its finality, the great weep of God.

The timeless oceans
course within us in our endless sighing,
our swallowing of ancient tears;
we breathe them through our briny lungs
until they dry,
until we die and sift our rime of salt
into the acid earth, and season it.

The sea,
the wide sea draws us back into itself,
down the long, slow rivers of its veins—
back into its hungry mouth again,

and the soul swims on
into the eye of God.

Jean Janzen

October

Now the blind for the hunters
is visible in the bare maple.
Last week your uncles hunched there,
listening among the rattle
of leaves. And the heart
of the deer was humming.

Today our feet swish through
the bright, fallen taffeta,
a cacophony before the slope
toward the barren stillness.
We can't save all the music.
The cabin is filled with antlers,

and how much can earth hold?
It's a matter of cadence
among extravagance.
Not hiding, but walking,
bold, into the death of summer
and into the clearing, singing.

Sara Covin Juengst
Going Home

Going home was a trip into quasi-familiarity:
    Remembered places and faces blurred by the patina of
        age;
I drove down our street:
    those sidewalks known from crack to crack
    that I still walk in my dreams;
    the neighbors' houses still the same after forty years of
        sheltering.
But other landmarks were gone:
    my father's workplace;
    the old hotel;
    Miss Eleanor's pillared home;
    the woods behind our house where bluets grew.
Resenting the newness that encroached on my memories,
I looked for the places that formed the borders of my life:
    the church: up for sale;
    the high school: new porticoes and rooms;
    Horton's Drugs: no soda fountain now;
    the house we lived in dressed in brick facade.
I long to pat it all back into the shapes I remember,
    but the kaleidoscope has shifted,
and only in my heart's eye
    will things forever be the same.

Autumn

My mother is shrinking inside her face.
A frightened child looks out
   from bleak, wide eyes.
Her glance wanders aimlessly
   over her book's pages.
She looks at me with a frail smile.
The energy that once was hers is stilled;
   she huddles in the big armchair.
She aches with perpetual pain.
She's there; she's not there.
Fading, shadowy,
   drifting quietly into another world.
It's hard to say good-bye to autumn leaves.

Neil Ellis Orts
House Blessing

"*D*aniel, a house grieves, too, you know," said Mrs. Hansen as she led the plumber to her bathroom. They were acquaintances, used to somewhat familiar conversation.

"How's that?" he asked.

"Oh, you know. Since my Harold died last spring, it seems the house has had to have so many little repairs." She showed him the problem with her toilet, and he set to work.

"What sort of repairs have you had to make?" he asked, turning wrenches and pulling parts.

"Little things, mostly. This old house shifted some this year, what with all the rain, so I've had to have work done on some doors and windows. Then there was a leak in the roof." She sat on the edge of the tub and played with her graying hair. "I keep telling the house to hold itself together, but it misses Harold, too."

Daniel smiled slightly. "Well, I imagine with Mr. Hansen gone, doors and floors and windows all get a little different use. That's what makes things fall apart." He was already finishing up. It was, indeed, a minor repair. "And you said yourself, the rains—"

"Yes, but it's more than that." He looked up, afraid she might be upset. Instead, he found her smiling. "You probably think I'm daft, but it's true. There's something about a house that misses people."

"I guess I don't know exactly what you mean."

She looked at the ceiling. "You've seen houses sit empty for just a little while but look like they've been abandoned for years?"

"Yes ma'am." He somehow felt it his duty to correct her thinking. "But like I said, when something gets used differently—"

"Nonsense. A house grieves." She noticed he had stopped working and had put away his tools. "All finished?"

"Yes ma'am."

"Write out my bill and I'll get my checkbook." They left the bathroom, she to her bedroom, he to the living room. He was tearing the bill out of his book when she walked in.

"It's the same with my children, you know." She took the bill and sat down at a small table to write her check. "They're just like this house. They try to be strong for me, but I know they have a break-down every once in a while, too."

"I guess it's hard," Daniel said.

"Yes and no. It's a comfort really, to know that I'm not the only one who misses Harold." She tore the check from her checkbook and handed it to him. "Expensive sometimes, but a comfort all the same."

Their business was completed with a handshake and well wishes, smiles and nods. She waved from her porch as he drove off in his old pickup. Then she went inside and gently closed the door.

Bard Young

Savor

"For everyone shall be salted with fire. . . ."
—MARK 9:49, KJV

"Ye are the salt of the earth," the preacher read.
I thought of white chunks in hot
dry desert, buried under stones, in sacks, in tombs,
the dried trace of tears down cheeks,
the gargle, deep in flu, deep in bed.

"The preacher meant salt as spice, for taste,"
my mother said. I thought of green beans
without any, of sliced tomatoes without any,
of boiled corn without any. It seemed right to me
that something good be loved when erased.

In Leviticus, priests in careful measure,
sacrificing meat to God—the temple thick
with holy fog that burns the eyes—
salt the smoking flesh, not for preservation
but for God's pleasure.

Something in salt is also pain.
I knew this as a child and worried.
The desert and the tears, the flu, the smoking meat,
those Levites living in the burning fog—
without salt, in earth, in me, what remains?

I wondered, how does God almighty face
the pleasure in the world,
the salted, smoking world,
its swollen knees and holocausts?
What absence of—what searing joy in—grace.

Gretchen Sousa
a daughter's terrain

my daughter
would rather have been born
a dog   a bear   a deer
than a girl disabled
different
from her sisters
keeps her drapes shut
prefers living in a cave
where she's invisible
she entertains
her hamsters   bird   iguana
in this darkened living room
green turtles moving slowly over stones
and one another
in their dim aquarium
the thin black cat
climbs my daughter's legs
sharpening her claws
on her jeans
the cocker spaniel watches

my daughter says
that within herself
she's hollow   empty   cannot find
enough trees   streams
and trustworthy creatures
to fill the   wide   open   spaces
inside her heart   those dry plains
that bowl of dust
is there a river
underground tributary of wet

and wild that winds its way unnoticed
into the mild days
and nights of her life
is there a love so potent
that a seed will grow
in a vast untapped desert   I see
a watery shape on the horizon
walking toward her   not on
    waves
but in a penetrating mist
that   lifts   and   fills
creates pools   rain forests
jungles

Frederick Buechner

Ted Schroeder

On my father's last dawn
I remember he opened the door.
I remember he closed the door.
I remember no thing he said if he said
a thing. Good-bye, boys.
Teddy and Billy, good-bye.
I am going downstairs.
I am going to turn on the car.
I am going to sit on the running board
and hold my head in my hands.
The two terrible women I love
will look after you. Your mother
will be a good mother but beware
of her tongue. Your grandmother
will pay the bills but beware.
I have left your mother a note only she will find.
I have showered and shaved.
I have combed my hair in the mirror.
I have dressed in clean clothes.
Your mother is still asleep in her bed
or pretending to sleep. As I passed
my mother's door I could hear her dreaming.
I have opened your door at the top of the stairs.
Now I will close your door and go down
in my gray slacks and maroon sweater,
my fresh shirt, my hair damp from the shower,
my note on the last page
of the book your mother is reading,
and start up the Chevy and wait
'til it gets me where I'm going.

Boys, I can leave you only the world.
I can leave the world only you.
Go away from this house.

Kate Benedict

Knees

And so I am brought to you again.
In this posture, on this gravel floor,
all my bones are numbered.

The pieties of childhood, the bedtime prayers,
have nothing to do with this ignoble humbling.

A sorrowful mystery, this.
There was a woman, once, whose grown son
was tortured before her eyes.
O son my soul,
I observe an agony—
disgraceful falls,
vinegar to drink, ridicule.
Then the nailing to the wood
and total paralysis.
By whom am I forsaken?

Despair is an extravagant word—
part sigh, part shriek—
but the experience, the thing itself,
is a numbness married to a clawing.
You rake your arms,
you rake your eyes,
you labor to uproot sensation,
buried deep.

Buried deep, all rectitude.
Buried deep, all hope.
Encrypted.
Sealed behind a massive stone.

I genuflect in the sepulcher of my life.
I kneel, but I do not keen.
The silence here is absolute.

Absolute, the darkness.
Resolute, the worm's tooth.

Ivy Dempsey

Alone

A broken and contrite heart, O God, thou wilt not despise.
—PSALM 51:17, KJV

Who is here?
I think it is I
who waits,
but it is more as if
something must rise through
a dark water. Water that is
a heavy life.

Sense of plants in orderly rows.
I need to go there. I need
to be
out.

Desperate yearning—
a trail of footprints left open
and dark in the snow.
Tree branches overhead, the gray
bark holding threads of tiny frozen
crystals. Will I last
this winter?

Armies mass on an ancient field,
horses distraught by the sound of
swords. Cries of the dying.
The dead.

Words like wounds. Words
impaling me for my
ignorance, sloth.

What I cry for
cannot be given
by anyone I see.

L. Jonathan Saylor
Flowing Music and Eternal Rest

*I*t can be extremely difficult to describe music and its impact on us for the simple reason that music can only fully define itself—it exists and evolves on its own and cannot be confined to the specifics of verbal description. Nevertheless, we are constantly trying to describe what we hear in music as a means of conveying, and in that process, exploring what music is and how it engages us as performers and listeners. Probably the word most often used in our attempts to describe music is *flowing*. It would seem to come closest in conveying the sense of inevitable, inexorable motion that is crucial in music making; for as so often noted, the dimension of time is music's "canvas"—the parameter it needs to function.

The term *flowing* also draws parallels in our minds to moving water, and it is perhaps no coincidence that music has been so often intimately tied to water. One thinks immediately of works such as Beethoven's *"Pastoral" Symphony* [#6] (second movement, "Scene by the Brook"), or Schumann's *"Rhenish" Symphony* [#3], inspired by the great Rhine river, or Debussy's great symphonic portrayal of the sea, *La Mer*. Perhaps one of the most effective and powerful evocations of water and its movement, via music, is Bedrich Smetana's tone poem *Vltava* (Moldau), where the composer deftly portrays this great river's journey through the Slavonic countryside in specific detail (made explicit through Smetana's own written descriptions).

While we rejoice in the intricacies of these ties—in the rippling flutes and clarinets depicting the gurgling spring generating Smetana's river—we perceive yet deeper connections. Flowing water also brings to mind tears, whether they be of joy or sorrow. Indeed, one of the most famous art songs at present dates from a collection of lute songs published in 1697: John Dowland's "Flow, My Tears," or "Lachrimae." Tears, of course, seem especially suited to music, for in their flow resides deep emotion—emotion often impossible to describe, yet at times given voice and expression through music.

It is in this context that we think of the great *Lacrimosa* movement of Mozart's *Requiem* (1791). Mozart is known to many today through that distorted yet stunning film Amadeus, where the moving strains of his *Lacrimosa* are played as his coffin is being carried to its anonymous grave site. For indeed, Mozart's last composition was his *Requiem*, a work he left unfinished. In fact, it was precisely measure eight of the *Lacrimosa* where Mozart stopped, unable to continue further. The irony of composing a mass for the dead as he lay dying did not escape the composer who remarked in a letter that it seemed he was composing his own funeral dirge. The *Lacrimosa* is verse 18 of the 20-verse *Dies Irae*, or "Day of Judgment," which traditionally starts out in a forceful and striking style (e.g., Verdi's *Requiem*). By the time we reach the *Lacrimosa*, however, the tone is much more subdued and even fearful. Here the text pleads for mercy as we face judgment and are to realize the full extent of our shortcomings: "Ah, that day of tears and mourning! From the dust of earth returning. Man must prepare himself for judgment." Mozart's *Lacrimosa* is filled with musical sighs and mournful ethos. One of the most powerful recent performances of the work was conducted by Zubin Mehta a few years ago literally inside the ruins of what had been the library in Sarajevo, Bosnia, destroyed by a tragic war—a cruel reminder of the tears shed as a result of our broken nature this side of eternity.

But these tears are not the end; the *Dies Irae* concludes with the *Pie Jesu*, which instills in us the hope that comes in Jesus: "Lord, all merciful, Blessed Jesus, grant them Thine eternal rest. Amen." While Mozart did not live to include the *Pie Jesu* in his *Requiem*, we do find it in the *Requiem* by the French composer Gabriel Fauré, dating 1888. Fauré's lovely movement for solo soprano wonderfully evokes the peace and deep joy of having been reconciled with God and being able to look forward to eternal rest in Him. Listening to this beautiful music, or to the waves reaching the shore gives us, just perhaps, a brief taste of what that rest must be like.

Bard Young

Loss of Memory

(Epiphany 1991) *

Eager in our souls, a brooding force—
huge and thrilling like a bird of prey.

It soars hawk-like, hungry and alert
    absorbing light, a shadow on the sun
        forming its trace below.
Behold the shadow circling in the light
    now rising, now descending, diving, closing
        on the newborn recollection.

    The rendered memory of the past
like steaming flesh new-torn from forming bone
cools, dries, then feeds the wide-winged shadow
    circling above and vigilant.

Recollections cannot fully form—
    of how we time and time again
        set fire to ourselves, the world.
Hungry for the issue of the past,
    alert for sinews of the recollection,
        comes the huge and hungry thrilling force:

Behold, the taloned spirit
who tears away the memory of the world.

Editor's note: On Epiphany, January 6, 1991, the United States stood at the brink of what was to be known as the Gulf War between the United States and Iraq over Iraq's invasion of Kuwait.

Carlene Hacker

The Silent Burn

For Lynn

Just yesterday our fingers ran the water's edge;
the breath of salt lay on our tongue.
We soaked in sun upon the shore
and felt liquid life flow over us.

Night comes too quickly.

The wind howls; the gulls beat their wings
like whips; the sea roils. Waves run wild.
They gather weight, lunge
upon the shore, and with a pull
as fierce and certain as a shark's jaw,
all we cherish is gone . . . taken . . .

simple things we held dear:
grains of sand, shells,
sight of a bird's smooth sail,
a small castle made together.

If it were not for hope, the silent burn
too deep for the eye to see,
the mind to dismiss, the sea to consume,
we would be lost
to life's wash. But in the heat
of hope, the gull glides again
and soars, the sea rests, and sand
like old lace sifts through fingers.

Nothing dies.
Rekindled, it flames.

Ivy Dempsey

A Singing

The singers and the dancers will say,
"All my fresh springs are in you."
—PSALM 87:7, BOOK OF COMMON PRAYER, 1977

O wrap us in death,
in the lightning-flash truth
that we are born
to die—

that this is a generous
destiny, that we should praise you
for our reliable
fate:

not doomed to huddle always inside
darkening rooms of these bodies staunch only
in their faltering
mortal ways,

but rather traveling at last with them,
each cell obedient, right in its work,
deep into another country
where you, our mercy, wait

to capture us, to pardon relentlessly
our stubborn resistance, our long
impassioned loyalty
to despair: its grim

suppression of the naive language
of our flesh; its ancient plan
of war—the iron and constant
will to give

ourselves away, one morning after
one morning, in burning rays
of a sun that is dying
with us,

to the fierce, nearly perfect desire
to keep always proudly alone.
However desperate.
Sad.

Gretchen Sousa
Elegies

I don't remember where we were
so long ago . . . Cuernavaca,   Guanajuato?
Leaning over the balcony
of a small hotel.   It was late,
late at night,
shadows dark in the plaza below,
amber lights glowing
on the old church.

I remember a sudden wind
lifted my hair
and your hand . . . there . . .
on the back of my neck.

I was once the bird
that flew against transparent glass,
knowing nothing of windows,
and with broken wings,
fell into another realm,   falling,
falling,
calling out to the one I longed for,
to be the sparrow in His hand.

Wait for me.
I go home to bury my dead:
regrets breathing their last,
memories stashed in boxes in the attic.
But grief,
that old acquaintance,
I shall keep with me always —

a molten river of gold
that streams
over the forge of my heart,
a fierce aloneness
that establishes us without malice.

May it burrow deep
into my soul
as I awaken to the listen
of mourning—pathway of grace,
to the sound of the hours,
while we are slow-danced across the
stage
like stars
in our radiant scarves.

Carlene Hacker

In the Absence

Day after day I look into the silence,
hoping for a whisper,
an assurance of what I already know.

Outside in the back yard,
a breeze brushes by, and I become aware
of hummingbirds,

ripping the air to shreds
and draining
one honeysuckle after another.

Tyrannical thoughts assemble
around the edges, eager
to snatch and steal these

small moments. I have been here before—
in these faceless spaces,
feeling liquid sipped from my veins,

awaiting transfusion, strumming
my thumbs at the long delay,
settling for quiet beauty,

for being alive
and listening . . .
listening.

Kathleen Long Bostrom
How Long, O Lord?

—*1 KINGS 18:21*

How long, O Lord,
　　shall we think of you
　　　　as some divine trickster
　　snatching from us
　　　　the lives of loved ones
　　　　　　as if you gained some glee
　　　　　　　　in our sorrow?

How long, O Lord,
　　shall we see you
　　　　as some heavenly dump truck
　　heaping loads of disasters
　　　　upon our weary shoulders
　　　　　　as if your goal was to try
　　　　　　　　to find our breaking point?

How long, O Lord,
　　shall we consider you
　　　　as some celestial child abuser
　　inflicting undeserved pain
　　　　upon your helpless children
　　　　　　as if your sole purpose in creation
　　　　　　　　was to find an outlet for your wrath?

How long, O Lord,
　　shall we go limping about
　　　　with two opinions?
Either you are a conniving, vengeful God

full of anger and hate,
Or you are a loving God
    who grieves with us in our losses,
        who offers to relieve our burdens,
            who cherishes each of us as a beloved child.

Give us wisdom to decide
    which God we choose
        to follow.

Bud Frimoth
Brittle Harp of Ice

Brittle harp of ice
    what is your music today?
Do you have a special melody to play
    which my ears need to hear
Or do you just play for sheer enjoyment
    in your momentary span of life?
    a song of beauty
    a tune of crisp delight
        that comes only by freezing
        droplets of melting snow.
You pluck the chords of morning sunlight
    and make a melody—
You pause at night to crackle your own
    ice harmony with the wind
    occasionally changing the key
    when one note strikes another
    shattering one piece of your icy string.
Oh that the coldness I often feel within
    could strum a simple melody of hope
    into this world of frightening speed
    and merciless isolation.
    Brittle harp of ice
    play your simple song within my heart.

Dean Blehert
Untitled

The Romans invented telephone poles.
Having no current, no wires, they
mounted men on the crossbars, lining
them up along the highways to shout the
good news from pole to pole.

Going Blind

Caravaggio's Peter, his face wrenched
by the stuttering violence of his words
aside into shadow, where no eyes
can hold him, denies and denies and denies.

A blackness blurs his fierce gleam.
It is agony to lie to whom but himself?

He wants to make someone not see,
            and you can see him going blind.

Carlene Hacker

The Promise

Still, there must be hope—
clearly as the full moon
perched at the edge of earth
just out of reach, but certain,
or the lake's wide stretch before me,
holding the silken glow
in its open palm.

The world
seems to have given up,
retired under its black cloak,
too heavy to lift its head
or even yawn. A weary giant,
its lands, races, creeds
thundering with rage,
exploding in flaming reds,
riotous violets, purposeless grays
while from the shadows,
children,
alone and crying.

Here at night, I hear the sound swell
like the heave and roll
of a slumbering beast
not yet silenced,
while the ball of light lifts
and rises through the dark
as if drawn by intention.

Clearly, there *is* more,
the full moon's promise,
There is father, mother.
There is peace. There is God.
Tomorrow's sun.

Kay Snodgrass
Power That Couldn't Fail

*I*n spite of severe thunderstorm warnings throughout the evening, a large crowd had assembled in our sanctuary for the memorial service of a dear church member, Sue. The rain that had been threatening all afternoon, managed to hold off until about five minutes into the service. I cringed as sharp thunder, then heavy rain, and even pelting hail mounted a counterattack on the pastor's quiet, but upbeat words. He told a story about a kite—weaving with this metaphor a word tapestry of Sue's light- and love-filled spirit pulling upward against the string that had anchored her to the earth. Half my attention, however, focused on pleading with God to please hold the storm off, at least until the service was over. A person gets only one memorial service, I thought; it shouldn't be like this.

Yet the longer the service continued, the louder the storm bellowed until by the closing liturgy, the noise outside drowned out the hundred-plus voices inside. Then just before the liturgy ended, a deafening peal of thunder shook the church, and all the lights went out except the ones for the emergency exit. With those, the minister had just enough light to continue the liturgy—alone.

Several of us seated in the back pews slipped out quickly in search of flashlights or candles. Using matches found in the kitchen, we searched the drawers and cabinets. The associate minister groped his way through the darkened halls to get some small and large advent candles. Once we had candles in hand, those of us who had set up the reception room earlier in Fellowship Hall placed the larger ones on the tables and serving bar and around the photographs of Sue, which her family had brought in before the service. The associate minister took the small candles and cardboard holders back to the congregation.

In a few minutes, all of the people in the sanctuary formed a candlelit processional toward Fellowship Hall. At first subdued, people gathered in small groups that rather quickly turned into lively conversation clusters, no doubt finding it especially easy tonight to talk about the weather. Some even joked that Sue, known for her vibrant personality, was getting our attention one more time. Instead of dimming our mood, the candles created a cheerful warmth and glow, not unlike that of a festive, candlelit dinner among friends or a blazing fire on a winter's evening.

Sue had died of cancer after a long, complex medical battle, a battle often pitting hope, courage, and medical wonders against spirit-drenching defeats. In spite of all their progress, science and technology had failed Sue at the last, just as they failed us that night in the church. And the storm had been mighty, mightier than all our earthbound powers save one—the power of people joined together, determined to celebrate Sue's spirit, which floated like a kite somewhere amid light and gentle breezes, and to help each other through the darkness.

Bard Young

The Yellowwood Tree

(Cladrastis lutea)

"Then the yellow tree of abundance was set up in the south as a symbol of the destruction of the world."
—Book of Chilam Balam of Chumayel

The Yellowwood was common once,
sometimes singly or in stands
along the forest's edge,
danced with blossoms whitely in late spring.

Yellowwood recedes now from the edge.
Summer leaves shadow its strength,
hard like smooth gray stone, strong
like the legs and curling trunks of elephants.
The close-grained heartwood, yellow sheen,
handled ax heads, gave them arc and speed
to chop even the gray-stone Yellowwood,
deeply bite the yellow heart
and echo rocks that fell like strokes of time.

Though harvest stopped, Yellowwood declines.
Remote in mountain valleys,
through fall while any green remains,
leguminous leaves feed on the air
as if it does not need the soil, the world.
And what of the world when Yellowwood
asserts its sign of absence beyond our seeing—
A Tree of Life whose arms grow dry and bare.

Kate Benedict

Contemplative Observances

Let this small apartment be a cloister
and me a pacing monk at morning prayer.

Let the windows of my ears shut against tumult,
let the tinnitus of garbage trucks be quieted.

The pure light of dawn suffuses the corridor.
Let my soul be thus illumined.

Let it darken also, for the maelstrom is infinite,
and the absolute an all-in-all of colors, a perfect black.

It's what I quail before, in my hooded bathrobe.
It's what body knows and un-knows. Knows.

My arms are open for a Pentecost.
I wait for tongues, a tribulation, the flame, the lamb.

I wait for the annihilation.
Let every sense and synapse acquiesce.

Reason has brought me here, the mind my beacon.
Reason will allow the exaltation.

Faith will accomplish it, one day.
As the carrion is taken by the vulture, I will be taken.

It will be all I hope for.
It will be nothing I hope for.

It is nothing I return to now.
A bare plank floor, a pall of dust.

And in each ball of dust, a galaxy of mites.
And in the essence of each mite: alpha, omega.

Shirley Klotz Bickel
Next of Kin for Three Persons

I

His skin balloon smooth
punctured by needles and
   vital hookups that
imprison this grown man on the gurney
headed for the operating room.
Sodium Pentothal deadened his will.
Legal documents signed away
   his rights.
"No admittance" signs will isolate me.
Yet I cling to the moving doctor's arm,
"But he's my son."

II

The Romans throw dice
for the garments I wove
not so long ago. I know
the mantle means nothing to them,
a moment's sport at the most.
If only I could have his mantle,
I'd wrap myself at night
and remember his growing-up days
before the miracles and crowds.
Still as a stone I am.
The soldiers ignore me,
this crazy woman
heaped on the ground
as if beseeching the "gods."
On my knees pleading, pleading.

Only God must hear my pleas,
"But he's my son."

    III

Without food for forty days,
tempted by Satan. Rejected
by religious authorities,
yet he never strayed from prophesy
he came to fulfill.
Now betrayed and forsaken
by those who knew him best.
He never harmed another being.
How could they condemn him to death?
Drop your whips, you
    puppets of power.
You've no right to tear his head
with thorns. Stop pounding nails
into his flesh. Give him a drink.
Don't leave him there
for vultures to feast.

You know not what you do.
I'll hide the sun and shake the earth,
rip apart the temple veil.
I'll open the tombs, and make
    the dead
to walk.
Clothed in darkness, perhaps
    you'll see,
"He's my son.
But he's my son."

Edward Wier
Sacrifice

If you had died an easy death I might have cried,
And grieved out all the suffering of loss.
Even Christ was wrapped and laid inside a tomb,
Taken down, after the burden of his cross,
With hope alive, still stretching out across

His death. Instead the sun rose on a dying day,
To burn my eyes and give my husk a glow,
A lesson learned without a crown or prize;
No gain of glory's risen scars to show,
A well completed sacrifice although

I live. No captive spirits freed from ancient chains,
Or Father pleased, awaiting my return.
No inspiration in my legacy,
Or hardened hearts to melt and then to turn,
With minds renewed to love, and hope to learn

Again. No witnesses to see justice unmade,
Or saints inspiring poetry and prayer,
To the God who still sustains my life,
For this reason men have called despair,
Where, only the sting of suffering I share,

With Him.

Lois Kilgore

Sonnet I

The few dead leaves still hanging from the tree
  Scratch helplessly, wind-tossed against the bark
  Of frosted branches winter-trimmed and stark,
Stiff relics left from summer's greenery.
Such freezing cold as knifes the flesh would be
  To men so bound more torment than their woe
  At wishing they could will themselves to go
Where other happier leaves lie peacefully.

This tortured grace God gives to those who fear
  His ever dimly known mysterious way:
Unending hours, imprisonment. They hear
  The call of love outside and far away.
No language but their clinging cry makes clear
    They only scratch the bark of any day.

Judith Deem Dupree
As an Eagle, Poised

[God] shielded him as the apple of his eye,
As an eagle stirs up its nest,
and hovers over its young;
as it spreads abroad its wings, takes them,
and bears them on its pinions . . . .
—DEUTERONOMY 32:10, 11

Above me, a dark bird hovers,
wind-spread, straddling the sky,
its beak a jabbing punctuation,
its voice a premonition rising
like a crest of wave before it.

Always we sense *You* there,
far beyond this small earth-huddle,
like a watchful shadow perched
within Your hidden solitude—
thrusting suddenly aloft, in grand
ascension, to hover, wind-spread,
on Your dark traverse of wing,
straddling eternity like a great
unfathomed presence, beak agape.

No prey are we who crawl across
the crust of this small circlet,
this, Your sacred lapis lazuli.
We are the apple of Your eye!
for lo, You have said it is so.

Yet our ears hear but a fragment
of Your call, and always the fear

of You spreads through our
rippling cells; the shiver of our
seeing You, seeing but the wild
of You, persists—an eagle poised
upside a brink unseen, crying
premonition to the labored earth.

Lois Kilgore
Still Light

Did you ever chase a firefly
Over shadowed dewy lawns?
Laughing, screaming at the beckoning
Twinkle as it led you on?

> I remember underneath the
> Giant Oak, I captured one,
> Bore it home, my cupped hands trembling,
> Bore it home, my light, my own.

> In a jelly jar with leaves and
> Bits of twigs and new-mown grass,
> Crawled my prize, his life slow-sifting
> Through his chambered hourglass,

> Dimmer, dimming—then we slept,
> And in the morning on a leaf
> I saw a beetle, stiff and ugly,
> Saw a bug and learned of grief.

Have you tried to bottle love,
Or tried to capture things that shine?
"God," I said, "my firefly died."
"Yours?" said God, "His light was mine."

LauraGrace Eisenhower
The Lost Word

"What brash, unmatched, egocentricity—
The time has come to end the myth with mind;
How could man be himself eternally?"
They said, and thus embraced faith redefined.

"That we should walk and talk again, what need,
When, adding their blessings to our best endeavor,
All memory, influence, even our very seed;
What need that we ourselves should live forever?"

And so they laughed and loved and lived their day,
And then one died. I heard the other pray,
Shaking the bars of his enlightenment,
He cried, "Can this be all? All glory spent?"
Beating his head against the wall of grief,
"Speak, speak, O lost Word, to my unbelief!"

Kathleen Long Bostrom
On Wings of Eagles

You perch on the edge
of my bed, ready
to fly, cradling my fingers
in your palm like a butterfly,
afraid to crush fragile wings.
Swallowed tears wash words
back down your throat, where
both remain, undigested.

Don't look at me like that,
seeing only death.
I'm living now, you're dying too,
but you don't know it.
The candle yet burns,
no longer a flame, but still
an ember glowing in the dark.
Do not extinguish me too soon.
And when the ashen wick
is cold and all that's left
a form of wax,
remember me, and weep not,
for I breathe free and soar
on wings of eagles.

Barbara Berger

Inheritance

What do the good souls leave behind
in crevices of hearts and minds
of those who grieve?

Is there a wealth of gold to mine,
inheritance for each to find
in memory?

God puts in all a spark, a flame,
which they can use to lift their name,
or servants be.

The well-used lives, the now chilled coals
have burned for other needy souls . . .
their legacy.

Judith Deem Dupree
O Dry Bones

When the world skims off and drops
like a stone spun out across the waves . . .

When we are forced back upon ourselves
by that mute gravity which tells us
that the grave will not redeem our souls
or crumbling bones . . .

when faith is but a tourniquet
to stanch the severed arteries that feed us—
that bleed our tainted blood across
the tainted universe . . .

when we have taken reasons—
plucked from the pruned, shaped flora
of our reasoning—
and shaped our rearrangements
to derangements that defile us,
that define us,
denying death when we have died
too many times,
too many ways to find our pulse again . . .

when we are one with the stars and stones
and plasma of those heavens,
strangely lifelike in our lifeless images,
our dry bones strewn across the valleys
of our darkened imagery . . .

when we have clattered to a fallen heap
full of final whimper at Omnipotence . . .

the universe shall hush, one startling moment—
one shivering, breathscape-moment from oblivion;

Ezekiel shall sing out, sing out, sing out,
and our bones will echo—rising, rising, rising!

Barbara Berger

Planting

The resurrection?

"Ah, yes,
Imaginative—
comforting
to those
who must
have hope,
have faith,
as the shovel
turns dirt
to plant
the dead."

My spade
invades earth
growing cold,
and dead stems
are forgotten
as brown bulbs
are buried
in dark places—
as hope,
as faith,
remembers Christ
and
plans a
resurrection.

IV. Waters of Restoration

*The Lord is my shepherd; I shall not want. He maketh me
to lie down in green pastures; he leadeth me beside the
still waters. He restoreth my soul . . . .*
—PSALM 23: 1–3, KJV

My God and Lord:
eyes are asleep, the stars are setting,
Quiet are the movements of the birds in their nests,
of monsters in the seas.
And you are just and unchanging,
the Equity that never strays,
the Everlasting that will never pass away.
Kings have locked their doors
guarded by their strong men.
But your door is open to any who call upon you.
My God, each lover is now alone with his beloved.
And I am alone with Thee.
—Rabi'a, a female Sufi saint, eighth-century Persia (paraphrased
from translations)

Judith Deem Dupree
After the Flood

Along its crumpled banks
the river brawls and shoves,
shouldering at restraining roots,
whining for release.

Puddles ripple with brief,
teeming life, and grasses lift
and stretch again,
flagging down the pulsing sun.

Sparrows clique and preen upon
the eaves and steamy cupolas,
welcome as the dove at Ararat.
Their fickle patter soothes the land,
still rheumy with its weeping.

Our aching throats unfurl
and open, bursting their tightness
like swelling stamens.

We breathe the primal air
in starving gulps, receiving
its new innocence, swallowing
our crumbled clots of grief.

We have left the ark,
the dark womb of our fear,
and stand, bruised
as the matted earth, drowning
in a sudden wave of joy . . .
consenting, at last, to death—
to new, uncertain birth.

Frederick Buechner
The Story (An Excerpt)

*T*he story that each of us has to tell is the story of a sacred journey in the sense that if I believe anything in this world, I believe there is no place where God speaks more eloquently to us than through what happens to us, and therefore our stories are sacred stories. And I think our stories are sacred also because they are, in a way, the Biblical story, which is a story that can be simply stated:

God creates the world, the world gets lost, and for the rest of the time, God tries to restore the lost world to Himself. That is the story of Israel, and it is also the story of you and me.

Dean Blehert
Tricks or Treats

On the way home, I bought Halloween candy,
but I was too late: I've given away two pieces,
eaten two, and I never did light the pumpkin.
I'm listening to the Grosse Fugue, and no one's
knocking at the door. By now
all the witches, ghosts, and monsters
that haunt our streets have become
children again. Christ said
none could enter in except
as children. Does this mean
no more masks, come as you are?

Or that we must wear our masks as
children do: For the fun of
surprised recognition? Ah! Yes, I
caught you, Beethoven, hiding in that
convoluted filigree the stern visage
of the opening theme; go on—dodge
behind a slow dirge and mock me from
the cello when I pursue the violin—
you can't get away—there! Got you!
Silence. The ghosts are on tiptoe.
Would you like an Almond Joy,
Little Ludwig?

Linda Malnack
Condemnation's Grip

Bubbles rise. Under the surface
an adulteress mouths the sinner's
prayer again and again for the same
sin. Her hair probes the current
like supplicating fingers. Her face
turns blue, gray. She doesn't see the lie
that holds her under, can only intone
her *sorry*s to the sea, to Jesus. And He
forgives, but she won't forgive herself;
condemnation chokes her walk,
clouds her view. Yet she looks up,
and specks the size of mustard seeds
shine in her eyes.

     She begins to see
condemnation's grip, the open door
that let it in, deformities it caused
in her life. Truth is a simple, sharp
blade, a voice in her watery wilderness
that tells her, *cut off the lie.* Desperate
for breath, she slashes. A thousand
black Beelzebubs flee, dark visions,
dark voices washed away, and in their
place a burst of air, a bright, new light
on the surface of water, wide enough
to walk on. She walks with Jesus.

Geoff Pope
Every Drop

Early in the morning
old music flies awake
holding new notes of faith
in the room of the meek
musician.
Covers off,
feet meeting the floor,
arms rising,
praise building,
he plants prayers
in the air,
moves
resurrection-ready
sliding up
scripture pictures
permanent on the walls
of his rejoicing heart.
"Worthy is the Word," he sings,
his cup of life overflowing
with the name of Jesus
written on every drop.

Carlene Hacker

The Journey

Away from the river's current
where others drift together,
washed by the rush of water
we knew would never cleanse us,
we grasp the jagged rocks,
mount the shore, and stand

alone,

drying wide open
in late October winds, watching
what we thought we needed
fall like leaves from autumn trees
and tumble downstream

We climb the cliffs
to higher ground,
where we are never less alone
than when alone

Later,
there will be others.
Now, holding nothing,
we are washed by choirs of silence
where we learn to live
with a soundless song.

John C. Purdy
Sweet Mystery of Love

Simone Weil adored George Herbert's poem "Love." She copied it in her notebook; she memorized it. Once, as she was reciting the poem, she had this experience: "Christ himself came down and took possession of me. . . . I only felt in the midst of my suffering the presence of a love, like that which one can read in the smile on the face of a beloved."

I read this vignette in Leslie Fiedler's introduction to Weil's *Waiting for God*. I copied the poem, carried it in my wallet, and memorized it:

Love bade me welcome, yet my
  soul drew back,
    Guilty of lust and sin.
But quick-eyed Love, observing
  me grow slack
    From my first entrance in,
Drew nearer to me, sweetly
  questioning,
    If I lacked anything.

"A guest," I answered, "worthy to
  be here."
    Love said, "You shall be he."

"I the unkind, ungrateful?
  Ah my dear,
    I cannot look on thee."
Love took my hand, and smiling
  did reply,
    "Who made the eyes but I?"

"Truth, Lord, but I have marred them; let my shame
    Go where it doth deserve."
"And know you not," says Love,
    "who bore the blame?"
"My dear, then I will serve."
"You must sit down," says Love,
    "and taste my meat."
So I did sit and eat.

In all of English literature, I have not found a more profound expression of the experience of grace.

I quoted the poem in a book about Jesus, in a chapter on the Foot Washing. I said it expressed the surprise and shock Peter must have felt when his master knelt to wash the dirt from his feet.

Soon after sending off the manuscript to the publisher I got a surprise of my own. While sitting in church, listening to Herbert's poem sung as a tenor solo. I thought I heard Ed Esposito sing:

Love bade me welcome, yet my soul drew back,
    Guilty of *dust* and sin.

I took a quick look at the bulletin, where the text of the solo was printed. It read, "Guilty of dust and sin." What had happened to *lust*? Was the church secretary guilty of a typo? After the service I went to the choir room and got a copy of the sheet music. There it was again, "Guilty of dust and sin," it read.

I photocopied the poem from Fiedler's introduction and sent it, and the church bulletin, to Martin Marty at the *Christian Century*. In a column devoted to "howlers," he printed my submission. He added some appropriate comments about Presbyterians in Ridgewood, New Jersey, with dusty souls.

Now the plot thickens, and the mystery deepens. Soon after Marty's column appeared, I got a letter from my copy editor. He had checked my manuscript against a collection of Herbert's poems. The original version of "Love" begins:

Love bade me welcome, yet my soul drew back,
   Guilty of *dust* and sin.

I went to the library and looked up a collection of Herbert's poems.
My copy editor was right. Fiedler—or his copy editor—was guilty of
swapping *dust* for *lust*.

But was Fiedler the guilty party? Perhaps Simone Weil had made
a mistake in copying the poem into her notebook. She was a French
woman, writing down a poem in English. Besides, a handwritten *d* is
not that much different from a handwritten *l*. Was it possible, as my
copy editor had suggested, that Fiedler had given his readers the version that Weil, herself, had known? Was it possible that in reciting
"guilty of lust and sin" she had felt forgiven? If so, in my book did I
want to stick with Weil's version?

Before I resolved that dilemma, the latest issue of the *Christian
Century* arrived. Some George Herbert lovers had written to Marty,
calling him to account for a "howler" of his own. Marty confessed his
carelessness in not checking the quotation from the Ridgewood
church bulletin with the original.

Who started all of us on this life of literary crime? Weil? Fiedler?
His copy editor? The mystery seemed insoluble. But before I answered
the letter from my copy editor, the mail brought a new biography of
Simone Weil by David McLellan. In the book were several photographs. One was of the page in Weil's notebook where she had copied
down Herbert's poem. There was no mistaking her handwriting. It was
clearly "dust and sin." Fiedler—or his copy editor—bore the major
guilt. Marty and I were culpable of not checking sources.

This was all recently recalled for me. Our adult Bible study class
had a spirited discussion of the forgiveness of sins. Near the end of the
hour, our leader, Henry, looked at his watch. Time to sum up. What
he believed about forgiveness was in a poem by George Herbert, he
said. And then he recited the poem, choking on the final lines. "I
always do that," he admitted.

And I confess that tears started up in my eyes as well. For some mysterious reason, I could hear my grandmother singing, "I love to tell the story . . . of Jesus and his love."

Several weeks after that adult class, I was in Manhattan for an Off-Off-Broadway opening of *Someone Who'll Watch Over Me*. I had a small financial and a huge emotional investment in the play: Our youngest son, Thom, was one of the producers, as well as one of the three actors.

After years of small parts and little theaters, he was finally on 42nd Street. He played the part of an Englishman who is taken hostage in Lebanon and imprisoned in a cell with an American and an Irishman. After the American is killed, the Englishman consoles his friend with Herbert's poem "Love." When Thom began to recite, "Love bade me welcome . . ." it was, for me, a moment of grace such as I have seldom known.

Again, I wept.

Geoff Pope

Preparing for La Push

For Dad

God said, "Labor to enter into that rest,"
So I try to relax and take a nap . . .
but end up with a map of the Northwest.

I settle on the Olympic National Forest.
Ironically, along the coast there's a place
called La Push. *Push* is the last word

I want to see, but it becomes easy to erase
the stressful reference, then imagine a bird
pushed back by a wave on the shoreline.

We will walk in the long light of August,
tasting the slow day, feeling that divine
nature, celebrating the everlasting trust
we have in the One who first imagined us.

Geoff Pope

Ocean Sign

"Crown him with many crowns . . ."
— MATTHEW BRIDGES (1800–1884)

It's the second day at sea,
and I'm squinting under the influence
of the West Indies sun
now transfiguring the main deck.
About 100 feet below the railing flows
the continuous fizz of the ship's wake.

I just saw something out in the water —
something small, floating . . .
now gone. It looked like
a little toy crown, perhaps
thrown from a past ship,
or lost from some land.

No, that's not it — I see
another adrift, and there's
another. They *are* crowns,
but weren't made by man,
not cut from cheap plastic;
they're seaweed . . . algae.
The water wears these
seaweed wreaths, these
algae crowns on Easter Eve.

Sara Covin Juengst

Viriditas

(To Hildegard of Bingen)

I look up at greening:
   trees dancing their intense songs,
   grasses curving over themselves,
   heart buds unfolding.
God is touching,
      breathing,
         speaking
            creation into abundance.
The radiance around is a spark
   to my dulled spirit.
I spring into life—
   one with the scent of rosemary,
      the laurel blossom cup,
         the cautious goldfish drifting.
Here is God's place for me.
I am gentle here.

Kathleen Long Bostrom

Sonrise

It was supposed to be
an Easter sunrise service down
by the lake, a gentle gathering
of the faithful singing praises
to our Savior as we watched
the heavens lift the golden sun
from slumber and set it tenderly
upon soft clouds.

Instead, it rained,
not only rain but thunder
and lightning crashing and clashing
and interrupting that gentle gathering
of the faithful huddled in a dim
sanctuary singing praises but disappointed
in the change of plans over which
we had no control.
And as I listened to the thunder
roar and shivered in the flashing
light, the words of Matthew came
to me, that tell of how on that first
Easter morning, when the two Marys
tiptoed to the tomb, a gentle gathering
of the faithful, they were greeted by the
shuddering sound of an earthquake and
dazzled by an angel robed in lightning
who told them the news,
the good news,
the greatest news
that Jesus was not there,
he had risen.

Then I knew
    that our expectations had been
        shattered like the Marys',
            and in the earthquake
                thunder and blinding
                lightning the stone had been rolled
            away, the tomb empty—
    Easter had come.

And though we did not see
    a sunrise on that wet and
        rainy Easter morn
            we, that gentle gathering
                of the faithful, heard the roar
                of angel wings and felt the
            Son rise in our soul,
    and we sang praises.
Alleluia! Amen.

Ivy Dempsey

New Mexico: The Visitation

All was taken away from you: white dresses, wings,
even existence.
—"On Angels," Czeslaw Milosz

I catch the hem
of the white robe
that is passé—after all, this is
the age of technology—

but I feel the grain
of your heavenly robe, in the tiny ridges
that mark my fingertips—
that make them real
to me.

It is all
a miracle—this becomes clear
after undeniable tragedy, after the demonic
cancellation of hope
has sheared the ordinary
from view.

The soft rosy light
now clasping the intense tops
of piñons in these mountains—
these Sangre de Cristos—oh sacred blood,
pour down, pour down
on me—

This connection: faltering, surprising,
thrilling—
the light: my eyes . . .

while I know certainly
my children will die—
I will die—
I cannot deny that this light
is heavenly. Of heaven.

Only you
can have told me.

Carlene Hacker
Memories through a Telescope

*F*or years, childhood memories of my father were best viewed through the large end of a telescope. It kept them at a distance. But recently, I believe God began urging me to turn the telescope around. Take a second look. Use a microscope to see what I might have missed.

I expected a rocky wasteland. I hardly knew Dad. After work and on weekends, he went to the tavern for "a drink with the boys." By the time he returned, alcohol often fueled him with a rage which swept like a violent storm through our house.

"Who do you think you are? You listen to me—" On and on he thundered, his face darkening, eyes glaring, each word a lightening bolt, striking, paralyzing, draining me of life. When he was finished, so was I.

Though terrified of my father, he was my world, my sun and stars. It was years before I told him, only months before he died.

I had worked through much of my past with a Christian counselor. Now to my amazement, reversing the telescope revealed long-forgotten memories. They appeared as flowers nestled between rocks, shapely shadows cast by the sun.

Among those memories were the stories Dad told on nights when rage didn't emerge. Hours after we finished dinner, Dad arrived home. Mom and I sat across the kitchen table from him. While eating, he told about his workday. I clung to every word. Listened to the tone of his voice for sharp-edged words or heavy breathing. But along with clues to the future of the evening, I learned about my father.

A mechanic for farm machinery, Dad had uncanny ability that was known by farmers from miles around. "Send Carl. No one else," farmers would instruct the company where Dad worked. Rich or poor, they called for "Carl." Dad, too, had his favorites.

Conditions in which Dad worked were often cruel. In the winter he worked outside in freezing temperatures, whipped by the wind streaking across open fields. Through the summer those same fields became ovens filled with steaming crops, dust, and blistering sun. But Dad loved the land. He understood it, respected it, and for the most part, the farmers who tended it.

There were farmers whom Dad didn't like. "They hire out the dirty work, then stand around to supervise. As if they *are* somebody," he snarled, swaying in his chair. "The rich hold tight to what they own. They wouldn't give you a glass of water if you asked for it."

Though Dad thought wealth was the problem, as a child I believed he sensed attitude, not bank account. Greed, pride — like the smell of unwashed socks.

Some flaunted what they owned. Seeing what they had, reminded him of what he lacked. Little self-esteem covered Dad's bones. They gnawed him raw. He let them know, smearing them with anger, searing me. *God, I don't want to be like those men and hurt people. Help me.*

A second telescopic look reminded me of rare stories which revealed Dad's soul. They involved farmers who lived simply and knew what it was to struggle, who seemed poor in spirit. With them, Dad touched something of heaven. He could put his "little" next to theirs. Through those stories I began to see shadows of beauty.

One night he said, slurring, "There I was in the blazing field under a filthy combine when Tom comes walking out with a tall glass of ice water for me. 'Here, Carl,' he says, 'I thought you might like a drink.' So I drank. He stood there and talked a minute or two. He told me, 'I'm sure glad you could come today, Carl. You make this job look easy.' Then he turned, leaving me to finish the job."

I remembered the flush of Dad's face. The sudden glisten of his eyes. The quick bow of his head as his fork toyed with food. "Can you beat that?" he asked.

Neither of us could. It was too great a gift for a man so poor.

Other times Dad told of farmers who invited him to come in for a cup of coffee after he worked until dark to finish a job.

"Did you go, Dad?" I asked, "Did you go in?"

"Naw. Not all covered with grease and grain. But it was nice of them to ask."

Sometimes he was rewarded after his work was finished. "The missus came out with a bag of potatoes and beans. She even wanted to shake my hand before I left."

"What did you do?" I asked, seeing the woman's hand extended to my father as if I were there. Imagining Dad's embarrassment, his quiet, sober smile. Dad was gentle when sober.

"I was full of grease. So I said, 'Gosh, my hands are all dirty,' but she just stuck out her hand anyway and said, 'We want to thank you, Carl.'"

Of course, Dad didn't go in. More than the grease, he couldn't shake off his inner emptiness. But they filled it some and he thanked them, taking away much more than vegetables for a job well done.

It seemed some people had something un-contrived that made him rich. As Dad spoke, I, too, drank of the love given to my father. Love that flowed from him as he told his tale. It warmed me as it warmed Dad. All the way down.

God, I want to be like those people. I want what they have. I want to give it to my father, to fill the void, to let him know that he is my world.

Now I needed a microscope to look into a past I had wanted to avoid. God showed me enough to make a wasteland bloom. I saw ways in which Dad and I were alike. The anger, resentment, and bitterness in Dad were in me. I, too, used them to cover years of pain. Only recently had I made changes toward healing.

The fear in Dad's eyes mirrored mine. The too-good-to-be-true feeling when something treasured is offered you. The apprehension that if you reach out, it will be snatched away, or if you try, it will disappear like a mirage.

Dad was afraid to trust. He, too, had been hurt. The love he and I craved as children had been denied, our hands slapped for wanting it. We held the same emptiness.

During those evenings, Dad looked like a frightened child. Just like me. His heart's barren field ached for a father's love. Not only a human father, but from the Father Who created him, knew his worth, and called him *good*. Just like me.

The major difference between Dad and me was that I had found God, found Him to be the Father with us, loving us in those childhood nights, wanting to be found, aching to wrap us in His arms.

In the midst of devastating rage, God had planted my wasteland. Now that I could see it, God seemed to say, "Take it home."

Remembering the farmers who didn't have much, still trembling with childhood fear, I gathered all that I could hold and took it to Dad now gentled by disease. There, with his "little" next to mine, Dad finally found God . . . his Father.

Carlene Hacker
The Wash of Water

It was one year after Dad died, just one year
since I'd seen his face too weak to turn
upon the pillow,
felt the almost-squeeze of a hand
which once held steel and made it bend,
heard the fight of phlegm within his throat,
each cough a struggle for life, for death.
Like a marathon runner pressing to the finish,
the opponent too close
to ease the pace, Dad fought
until he won . . .

one year to remember us as strangers
living under the same roof, chaos
threaded through flesh and blood
of separate souls in a single room,
hellish wars, the wounded
too incoherent to name wounds,
too frightened to hope for more,
too desperate not to try again . . .

one year to remember that before he died,
our hearts touched like magnets
held apart too long,
years of yearning reconciled . . .

one year,
holding fast the memory of our miracle,
I drove to the ocean
where they'd thrown his ashes
and watched angry waves
throw themselves upon a defenseless shore,

then collapse, recede, and try again.
I looked out past the violence,
past the peaceful waters we had known
for too short a time.
And I let it all wash through me.

Sunrise
Salty air
Beat of a gull's wing
God sighs
Smiles

Neil Ellis Orts

Dancing on My Own Grave

"What day is it?" the old man asked, barely opening his eyes.

"It's Sunday, Papa," answered the woman sitting beside his bed. "It's Easter Sunday."

He smiled, closing his eyes. "Christ is risen."

"He is risen indeed," she said without joy.

"Alleluia. You're supposed to say, *Alleluia*." He coughed.

"Alleluia, Papa."

"Are you going dancing? We used to have an Easter dance. Couldn't dance all Lent."

"No, Papa. I don't know of any dance today."

The room was silent again for a while.

"What day is it?"

"I told you, Papa. It's Easter Sunday."

"That's right, that's right. Christ is Risen."

She didn't respond until he opened his eyes and looked at her.

"He is risen indeed." She rolled her eyes up into her forehead. She didn't mean the word. "Al-le-luia." She drew it out because she couldn't say it fast.

The old man closed his eyes again. Smiling he told her, "Take my hand."

She did.

"Withered isn't it?" He laughed and then coughed a bit. "Even when it was fat and plump, it was just dust hiding dry bones. Dust and dry bones." He fell silent. Again, he asked,

"What day is it?"

"Remember, Papa? Christ is risen?"

"He is risen indeed. Alleluia. Yes, I remember." Suddenly, his eyes were wide. "You remember, too."

"Yeah, Papa. I'll remember."

"Then . . ." The old man stared at the ceiling. "Then I'll see you at the last. I'll be the one dancing on my own grave."

He closed his eyes, and, after a while, there came a rattling rush of wind from his chest.

Once she stopped crying, she got up to make her phone calls.

Judith Deem Dupree
All That Is

The heavens bend,
full and generous above us,
earth circling on its tether as it
ever has, while we in this small
garden unfold our petalled
souls and fall in silent drifts.

Here, the starlings circle,
orbiting the sun, gleaning over
close-cropped fields,
and eagles waver, sky-born,
riding August's heated air;
lizards flit across the crusty rocks
like unconnected shadows
while we are born and buried . . .

And I stand, now,
beneath this arching universe —
to hear the trees sing soft *Te Deum*,
to memorize the moon
caught briefly in its nest of clouds;

and I stand, wondering,
still *wondering* at all that is, and was —
the endless circle of our being,
and the endless fire of it —
the brevity and grand bravura
of His Flame within us.

Tributaries

And I heard a voice from heaven, like the voice of many waters, and like the voice of great thunder; and I heard the voice of harpers harping their harps. And they sang, as it were, a new song before the throne . . .

—REVELATION 14:2–3, KJV, ALT.

Kay Snodgrass
A Poem to Living Poems
In appreciation to the contributors to this anthology

Before light, before land
Before eye, ear, or heart of man,
I Am
Spirit over water
Darkness, deep and still
Expanding mind, swirling, swelling will
Heaven-making
Word over water
Splitting light from dark
Forming land from sea
Spinning sun and moon, lighting stars
Image over water
River outward flowing
Reflects a garden growing
A fish, a snake, a bird, a lamb
Eye, ear, heart of man,
A woman's voice to call
I Am
Singing over water
Songs of joy and laughter, greeting,
Poems of living matter.

About the Artists and Writers

KATE BENEDICT's poetry has been appearing in literary magazines and anthologies for twenty years.

BARBARA BERGER, poet, parent, and grandmother, has had her poems published in literary magazines and has been honored by the San Diego County Christian Writers Guild.

SHIRLEY KLOTZ BICKEL, a piano teacher and a director of Christian education who has published extensively, is married to a Presbyterian minister and is the mother of four children.

DEAN BLEHERT has had six books published, most recently *Please, Lord, Make Me a Famous Poet or at Least Less Fat*. He publishes a bimonthly "poetry letter" of his poems, *Deanotations* (for a free sample, write to *Deanotations*, 11919 Moss Point Lane, Reston, VA 20194, or visit the Web site: http://www.blehert.com).

KATHLEEN S. LONG BOSTROM, a Presbyterian minister, is the author of *The World That God Made*, *Who Is Jesus?*, *What Is God Like?*, and *The Value-Able Child: Teaching at Home and School*, as well as prizewinning sermons and other works.

FREDERICK BUECHNER is a Presbyterian minister and world-renowned theologian, writer, and author of novels such as *A Long Day's Dying* and the Leo Bebb series, as well as nonfiction, including *The Longing for Home*, *The Magnificent Defeat*, *The Faces of Jesus*, and *Peculiar Treasures*.

IVY DEMPSEY has been publishing poems for some years in literary journals, teaching in universities, and conducting many poetry workshops, including some at Ghost Ranch, operated by the Presbyterian Church (U.S.A.), in Abiquiu, New Mexico.

MARY DUCKERT spent over twenty years of editing, writing, and teaching teachers of children for the Presbyterian Church (U.S.A.). She is author of *Help! I'm a Sunday School Teacher*, revised in 1995. Now retired, she edits, writes, consults, and does tutoring in English as a second language through her church in Portland, Oregon.

JUDITH DEEM DUPREE contributes poetry and prose to literary magazines and theological journals. She is founder/director of AD LIB Christian Arts, a retreat-based ministry, and of Master*s Class, a creative writing workshop (P.O. Box 365, Pine Valley, CA 91962).

LAURAGRACE EISENHOWER is a retired teacher who upon retiring became a Presbyterian minister. The widow of the Rev. Dr. William Eisenhower, and the mother of five children, she continues her writing into this, her eighth decade.

BUD FRIMOTH is a retired Christian educator and radio broadcast journalist, producer, and director of the Open Door Radio Ministry. He and his wife, Lenore, own and operate WD Productions, a clown ministry, along with "other creative endeavors," and have run Clown Funshops (workshops) in nine states.

NICORA GANGI is a noted artist and art teacher and lecturer who holds B.F.A. and M.F.A. degrees from Syracuse University. See her Web site at www.pulsar.org/gangi/gangi.html.

CARLENE HACKER has written for numerous publications. She won the San Diego Christian Writers Guild's Best Published Article of the Year Award in 1996 and 1998, and Best Poem of the Year Awards in 1987, 1992, 1994, and 1997.

JEAN JANZEN teaches poetry writing at Fresno Pacific University and Eastern Mennonite University in Virginia and has published five collections of poetry, the latest being *Tasting the Dust* (Good Books, 2000). She also won an NEA grant in 1995 and won the first-place award of the Associated Church Press for the poem "December 1941," published in the journal *The Mennonite*.

SARA COVIN JUENGST, a Presbyterian minister and certified Christian educator, won an award for the best Bible study in a denominational publication (*Horizons*) in 1996 and is the author of several books, including *Breaking Bread, Like a Garden*, and *Sharing Faith with Children*.

LOIS KILGORE is the author of an array of works, including *Eight Studies for Senior Highs*, a widely used enrichment curriculum for churches; and *Violence Against Women*, a recent study used by churches. She co-wrote *To God Be the Glory*, a film for the Grand Canyon Presbytery. She and her husband, a retired Presbyterian minister, raised nine children.

G. WILLIAM (BILL) LANKTON, pastor of two churches in Wyoming and Michigan and director of Presbyterian Camp in Saugatuck, Michigan, for twenty-four years (now retired) and a trained commercial artist, is married and the father of three children, one deceased.

ANGIE MAGRUDER, internationally known and commissioned artist from Reston, Virginia, paints and teaches painting in several media, especially watercolor, and previews her work on her website at: http://www.angieink.com.

LINDA MALNACK, whose poetry has appeared in various publications, including *Calyx, Christianity and the Arts*, and the *Seattle Review*, has also published a chapbook, *Bone Beads* (Paper Boat Press, 1997). She lives in Seattle, Washington, with her husband and three children.

MARY NELSON is a fine-art photographer who tries to capture a meaningful moment of peace and introspection in her photographs and who says her Christian faith affects all aspects of her life.

NEIL ELLIS ORTS holds a B.F.A. in theater from Southwest Texas State University and a Master of Divinity degree from the Lutheran Seminary Program in the Southwest, is the author of *Watch and Pray: Meditations for the Season of Lent in Dramatic Form*, from CSS Publishing Co., and has had articles published in a number of periodicals.

GEOFF POPE, whose poems have appeared in *Christianity and the Arts*, *Chronicles*, *Christianity and Literature*, *Radix*, and *Cornerstone*, was editor for the International Writing Program at the University of Iowa (1989–1993), and is now an assistant professor of English and creative writing at Dominion College in Seattle.

JOHN C. PURDY, a freelance writer and an educational consultant, is a retired Presbyterian minister and editor of educational materials for youth and adults. He is the author of numerous publications, including *Parables at Work*, two adult studies in the Kerygma program: *Lord, Teach Us to Pray* (a study of the Lord's Prayer), and *Blessed Are You* (a study of the Beatitudes), as well as several short-term Bible studies for Presbyterian Men, Presbyterian Church (U.S.A.).

L. JONATHAN SAYLOR is associate professor of music and head of the music history and literature department at Wheaton College Conservatory of Music, Wheaton, Illinois. He and his wife, Susan, have two daughters.

KAY SNODGRASS is the editor of *These Days*, a daily devotional guide and resource published quarterly by the Presbyterian Publishing Corporation. She also writes and conducts workshops on spiritual formation and devotional writing, editing, and reading.

GRETCHEN SOUSA, award-winning poet, is the author of four books of poetry. She has published in *Sojourners*, *Inklings*, *Mars Hill Review*, and *Encodings*, and leads the poetry workshop for the Christian Writers Guild Conference held annually in Del Mar, California.

JEANNE D. WANDERSLEBEN is a retired certified Christian educator in the Presbyterian Church (U.S.A.). She has written educational materials and has devoted much time to preserving and publishing the letters of her aunt, Edith E. Husted.

EDWARD L. WIER, whose articles, stories, and poems appear in various journals and magazines, is a professional musician, teacher, and freelance writer with a B.A. in theology. He has written music for national television specials and film, as well as publishing the CD *Mere Guitar* (Brio Records, 1604 Woodcliff Dr., Dunwoody, GA 30350).

BARD YOUNG, author of the award-winning novel *The Snake of God* (winner of the James W. Angell Award for best book by a Presbyterian) is the editor of Vanderbilt University Press and editor and director of the *Cumberland Poetry Review*, a widely respected journal of poetry and criticism.

TRINA ZELLE, a writer and Presbyterian (U.S.A.) pastor, also serves as Border Ministry Coordinator for Cristo Rey Outreach, Inc., a Presbyterian ministry in Sunland Park, New Mexico.